HERE'S TO YOUR HEALTH

Second Edition

DONNA BECK RICHARDS, R.N., M.S.

Dallas County Community College District

KENDALL/HUNT PUBLISHING COMPANY
2460 Kerper Boulevard P.O. Box 539 Dubuque, Iowa 52004-0539

Acknowledgments

No project like this can be completed by one person alone. There are a number of special people who deserve recognition for making this study guide a reality. Particular thanks to Ted Pohrte, Director of Instructional Services, for his encouragement and support, and for spending a part of his 40th year in education guiding this neophyte writer; Pam Quinn, Director of Educational Resources, and Bob Peterson, Director of Information and Distribution, for giving me the opportunity to do this project; Annette Milton and Janice Moss, Editors, Linda Sparks, Desktop Publishing, and Liz Gonzalez, Word Processor, for their part in making my handwritten, sometimes disjointed, copy into a coordinated whole; the members of the Here's To Your Health study guide committee for their leadership, particularly Avis Jamieson and David Gregory, with whom I have spent so much time "talking health" through the years; and Rodger Pool, Associate Vice Chancellor, for recommending me for this project.
-- **Donna Beck Richards**

The 25 television lessons of *Here's To Your Health* were produced by **KERA-TV, PBS**, Dallas/Fort Worth/Denton, Texas.

Dallas County Community College District
CENTER FOR TELECOMMUNICATIONS

Director, Educational Telecommunications: Pamela K. Quinn
Manager, Production Services: Robert Crook
Director, Instructional Services: Ted Pohrte
Director, Information and Distribution: Bob Peterson
Director, Business Services: Dorothy Clark

This edition has been printed directly from camera-ready copy.

In memory of

G. Gordon Beck

Leader, mentor, friend,

but most of all

my father

CONTENTS

TO THE STUDENT

"While science may help explain how a virus multiplies, it leaves unanswered why a tear is shed."

Bernard Lown, M.D.,
In Norman Cousins' *The Healing Heart*

Introduction

Welcome to the most important course you will ever take! If you don't agree with that statement, you may need to reevaluate your viewpoint upon completion of this course.

Ponder this. The human body is the most complex, efficient, low-maintenance machine ever created. Centuries of inventions and technologies have not come close to duplicating the complexity and efficiency of the human body system. Health is the most precious commodity known. There is nothing that can replace it, no substitute for it.

Unfortunately, we take our bodies and our health for granted. We assume everything will "work" throughout our lifetime until we die at a ripe old age. To illustrate: if we treated a car the way most of us treat our bodies, it would break down very quickly. Too often we just live from day to day, giving little thought to the details of our lifestyles that will have great impact on our future health and happiness.

Here's To Your Health is designed to help you define your lifestyle, make decisions about that lifestyle, and improve those areas of it that will bring you to a state of optimal health.

Don't limit yourself to the TV and textbook assignments. Read widely, but critically, about the subjects. Everyone has opinions about health, and although some are excellent, others are ridiculous. Select reading materials that are logical, workable, and suitable to your needs and values. Be suspicious of fads and off-beat ideas.

At this point you may be remembering those boring health and hygiene classes you sat through as a kid -- forget them! This course offers a new, innovative approach to the subject. Open your mind. *Here's To Your Health* will challenge you to "add life to your years, not just years to your life."

Health is not merely an absence of disease. Health encompasses all the aspects of physical, emotional, and social wellness. It should be a positive, creative force in our lives that enables us to achieve the things we want to do.

Such achievement, however, may not always easy. After all, anything that is worthwhile takes effort.

COURSE GOALS

Here's To Your Health offers you, the learner, an opportunity to examine all the factors influencing your health. This course is designed to give you the tools necessary for achieving and maintaining an optimal, healthy lifestyle.

These are the basic objectives of *Here's To Your Health*:

1. To increase your understanding of the elements that contribute to a "wellness"-oriented lifestyle.

2. To encourage you to take responsibility for maintaining your own health.

3. To help you understand the risks to your health and their potential for causing illness and even death.

4. To increase your knowledge of the most important health risks to the world's population.

5. To provide you with knowledge of the progress being made in science and medicine in the 20th century and to prepare you for the issues of the 21st century.

6. To broaden your understanding of the most frequently used treatment options available in medicine today.

7. To eliminate misconceptions, fallacies, and confusion you may have concerning modern health issues.

8. To aid you in understanding the role that government plays in the health of its population.

9. To instill knowledge that will help you be active in encouraging legislation that promotes the health of the population.

10. To encourage you to begin or continue optimal health practices that will serve as models for the generations to come.

TEXTBOOK

Levy, et al., *Life and Health: Targeting Wellness.* 1st Edition. Random House, 1991. ISBN: 0-07-037494-5.

STUDY GUIDE

To complete this course successfully, follow these guidelines when studying *each lesson*.

1. Read the Learning Objectives.
2. Read the Overview.
3. Study the reading assignment noted in the Study Assignments.
4. Look up the Key Terms in the textbook.
5. Answer the Text Focus Questions.
6. Watch the television program noted in the Study Assignments.
7. Answer the TV Focus Questions.
8. Complete the Optional Strengthening Exercises.
9. Take the Self Test.

LESSON 1   Why We're Killing Ourselves

"It is becoming more and more apparent that we rust out instead of wear out.   Physical and mental activity are vital if we wish to prolong the youthful portion of life and enjoy later years. "

Anonymous from *Winning Words*

Learning Objectives

Knowledge

Upon successful completion of all assignments in this lesson, you should be able to

1. Define health in terms of a balance between five distinct but interrelated dimensions.

2. Analyze the importance to health of the components of lifestyles as elements that can largely be controlled by individuals for the benefit of their health and feelings of self-efficacy.

3. Explain how health goals can be refined by relating them to needs and wants; personal goals, both short-term and long-term; and the priorities and trade-offs that can make an individual feel most comfortable.

4. Describe a process of setting health goals through realistic self-assessment.

5. Distinguish between the immediate effects of active involvement in health-enhancing behaviors and the long-term benefits that can be gained by changing health-related aspects of one's lifestyle.

1

6. Identify and describe both alterable and unalterable risk factors.

7. Describe the influence stress has on risk factors.

8. Discuss the changes in lifestyle that have occurred with each successive generation.

Attitude

1. Accept the concept of individual responsibility in maintaining health.

2. Commit to a "wellness" lifestyle.

Overview

Our lifestyle has evolved from that of hunting and gathering food to one of sedentary work and packaged edibles. At the same time, strides in technology have conquered many of the diseases that killed our ancestors. This sequence of events has created a major shift in the causes of illness and death in our population.

Until recently, our health was considered a matter of luck more than individual responsibility. Dreaded diseases were of bacterial or viral origin; their outcome was dependent on medical treatment and other factors largely out of the control of the individual. Now the diseases that kill us are more frequently chronic ones caused at least partially by our own lifestyle. In other words -- we may be killing ourselves!

If the idea of killing yourself is startling, consider the way America lives and then compare some of the major causes of heart disease and cancer. As a group we eat far too much red meat, fat, salt, and sugar. We don't exercise enough, and many of us smoke, drink too much alcohol, or use other chemicals that are harmful to our bodies. The good news is that all of us can positively impact our lives by making decisions to lower some of our risks and change our lifestyles to accomplish these goals.

Many of the positive changes we can make are small: using the stairs instead of the elevator, eating nutritious snacks instead of junk food, cutting our salt intake, and buckling our seat belts. Some are more difficult: losing weight, breaking a smoking habit, or beginning an exercise program. The important thing is that all these suggestions will make you feel good, look better, and be healthier. Best of all, you will be taking responsibility for your own wellness.

Study Assignments

Textbook - Chapter 1, "The Concept Of Health," pp. 3-27

TV - Program 1, "Why We're Killing Ourselves"

Complete the Self-Assessment on p. 11 in the text.

Key Terms

hardiness (textbook, p. 5)
homeostasis (textbook, p. 9)
regenerate (textbook, p. 9)
genes (textbook, p. 10)
lifestyle (textbook, p. 12)
self-efficacy (textbook, p. 17)
priority (textbook, p. 20)
trade-off (textbook, p. 21)
comfort level (textbook, p. 21)
lifestyle factors (TV)
risk factors (TV)

Textbook Focus Questions

1. How can you integrate each dimension of health into your own life?

2. How does lifestyle impact health?

3. What are the components of lifestyle and why are they important?

4. Explain needs and wants in relationship to Maslow's "hierarchy of needs."

TV Focus Questions

1. How have the diseases we die of changed through the years?

2. Name the major lifestyle risk factors, both alterable and unalterable.

3. Contrast our former lifestyle as "scavengers, gatherers, and hunters" with our present urban lifestyle.

4. Describe the role that stress plays in our lifestyle risks.

Optional Strengthening Exercises

1. After consultation with your physician and your instructor, begin a regular exercise program.

2. If you smoke -- STOP! (Additional information is in Lessons 20 and 21.)

3. Begin a plan to take stock of your own health. (textbook pp. 21-24)

Self Test

Take the quiz by marking the correct answer to each question. After item 10 use the Answer Key to check your answers. Review items missed to be sure you understand the correct answer.

1. The major causes of death today are

    a. typhus and smallpox.
    b. auto accidents and cancer.
    c. cancer and heart disease.
    d. all of the above

2. Stress impacts our lifestyle by influencing our choice of life habits.

    a. true   b. false

3. The Dimensions of Health include

    a. emotional, intellectual, and physical health.
    b. social and spiritual health.
    c. lifestyle only.
    d. a and b

4. Health is simply the absence of disease.

    a. true   b. false

5. The natural equilibrium the body seeks is known as

    a. regeneration.
    b. integration.
    c. homeostasis.
    d. none of these

5

6. Fortunately we can control all aspects of our health today.

   a. true   b. false

7. Some of the contributing factors in the increase of chronic diseases are

   a. urbanization, smoking, and diet.
   b. stress, increased exercise, and crowding.
   c. sedentary lifestyle, technology, and viruses.
   d. drugs, stress, and increased exercise.

8. We have little control over the major causes of death today.

   a. true   b. false

9. Needs for water, food, shelter, sleep, and human contact are _____, according to Abraham Maslow.

   a. basic
   b. higher level
   c. optional
   d. none of these

10. Most people concentrate on achieving short-term health goals, rather than long-term ones.

    a. true   b. false

Answer Key

1.   c (TV)
2.   a (TV)
3.   d (textbook, pp. 5-8)
4.   b (textbook, p. 5)
5.   c (textbook, p. 9)
6.   b (textbook, p. 17)
7.   a (TV)
8.   b (TV)
9.   a (textbook, p. 19)
10.   a (textbook, p. 25)

LESSON 2   Stress: Is Your Lifestyle Killing You?

"A wise man should consider that health is the greatest of human blessings, and learn by his own thought from his illness."

Hippocrates, *Regimen In Health*

Learning Objectives

Knowledge

Upon successful completion of all assignments in this lesson, you should be able to

1. Define stress as the body's response to perceived challenges or stressors, some of which may give rise to considerable achievements, others to withdrawal and even ill health.

2. Explain how the nervous system and chemicals in the bloodstream cause specific stress-related effects in the body that may lead to long-term damage if the stress is allowed to continue without relief.

3. List some of the effects that stress can have on an individual's life, ranging from self-destructive behaviors such as excessive drinking to long-term damage to vital body systems.

4. Describe different strategies that can be used to manage stress, ways to relax in the face of stress or to change one's perception of stressors, and approaches that give the body and mind greater resistance against stress in general.

5. Describe the relationship of personality type with vulnerability to stress-related illness.

Attitude

1. Describe signs that show you are under too much stress.

2. Develop a plan for coping more effectively with stress in your life.

Overview

When asked whether stress is good or bad, most students will say BAD without hesitation. The fact is -- if you do not have stress in your life, you are DEAD. Stress keeps us alive. Of course, stress has a significant downside, but the point is that stress is both good and bad. The ways by which you cope with stress determine whether it is a positive or negative force in your life.

In your TV lesson, Dr. Elliott Snyder described the three ways to look at stress. Each has meaning when applied to our own lives and the stresses we deal with: 1) external events trigger an 2) internal subjective emotional response, 3) causing the body then to experience the non-specific response called the general adaptation syndrome. Recognizing your set of reactions to stress becomes important as you learn ways to cope effectively with that three-step process. Most of us have fairly specific ways to react to stress that are repeated each time we experience too much stress. Once you begin to "read" your own actions more efficiently, you can utilize this knowledge to reduce stress in a variety of ways.

Of course, solving the problems causing the stress is the most desired and long-lasting solution to the stress issues in your life. However, there are some short-term "band-aid" solutions that are applicable. The simplest is stretching or moving around when you find that studying for that test or doing that other activity has made you tight and tense. Try taking a break and see if you notice a difference in how you concentrate afterwards.

A slightly longer lasting relaxation exercise is easily learned and quite effective. First, sit in a comfortable chair with your legs uncrossed, your arms in a relaxed position, and your eyes closed. (You may also lie down to do this exercise.) Begin by consciously relaxing your toes, then your feet, then your ankles, legs, and gradually every other part of your body. Once completely relaxed, in your mind's eye, take yourself on a mini-vacation to a favorite spot -- the beach, a mountainside, a flowering meadow, or some other happy place. Really experience the joys of where you are. Smell the salt air, feel the warm sunshine on your body and the sand under your feet, hear the sound of the surf and the gulls calling. Feel the stress melting away and stay in this fantasy place until you are ready to come back and cope. Again, this doesn't solve the problem, but the exercise gives you some breathing room and strength to cope with stress.

Another coping mechanism is to plan your life so that you have time each day for yourself. Some tend to think they have to pack 35 hours of productivity into each 24-hour period in order to feel worthwhile. This misconception is dangerous. Do some realistic planning so your goals can be accomplished (not completing things is stressful), and then take time to renew yourself. Don't feel guilty about it. The renewal process is important to avoid burn-out and other stress-related conditions. Take time for yourself and feel good about it!

To relieve some of the stresses of life, the problems causing the stress must be solved. Here again planning is of major importance. Take a careful inventory of those concerns causing stress in your life and separate those that you can't control from those that you can control. Put those you can't control out of your mind (worrying doesn't help). Then, decide on the importance of the remaining problems and work on them one at a time. It doesn't matter whether you solve easy ones first and then work on the difficult ones or vice versa. The secret is to work on one or two at a time and not try to solve all of them at once. Do not create a situation that is overwhelming and leads to greatly increased stress levels by trying too many tasks at once.

There are no instant solutions to stress problems. The text and the TV program discuss the theories related to stress and its effect on health and disease. In this overview are some simple exercises to help you bring theories and information together in a useful plan for coping with the stresses in your life.

Good luck! And remember: *you* hold the key to managing your own life.

Study Assignments

Textbook - Chapter 2, "Stress And Its Management," pp. 29-51

TV - Program 2, "Stress: Is Your Lifestyle Killing You?"

Complete the Self-Assessment on pp. 34-35 in the text.

Key Terms

stress (p. 30, TV)
stressor (p. 30)
eustress (p. 33)
distress (p. 33)
general adaptation syndrome (GAS) (p. 33, TV)
endocrine glands (p. 36)
hormones (p. 36)
Type A personality/behavior (p. 39, TV)
Type B personality/behavior (p. 39, TV)
progressive relaxation (p. 45)
relaxation response (p. 46)
autogenic training (p. 47)
biofeedback (p. 48)
cognitive appraisal (p. 48)
epinephrine/adrenalin (TV)
hypertension (TV)

Text Focus Questions

1. What are the general categories of stressors that affect us and how can each be defined?

2. Discuss the general adaptation syndrome as described by Dr. Hans Selye.

3. Describe the responses of the various body systems to stress.

4. How do Type A and Type B behavior each relate to coping with stress?

5. How does increased stress affect behavior?

6. What role does stress play in disease?

7. Describe some techniques used to manage and reduce stress.

TV Focus Questions

1. Discuss three ways to look at stress as suggested by Dr. Synder.

2. What are some of the most common symptoms of stress?

3. Discuss the probable relationship between stress and disease.

4. Compare the Type A personality with Type B.

5. What are some of the effective treatments for individuals having problems with stress?

Optional Strengthening Exercises

1. Develop a list of positive and negative stressors in your own life and make some plans for coping with these.

2. Learn and practice one of the relaxation exercises.

3. List some advertising devices that seem to employ "rip-offs" or quackery in advertising products designed to reduce stress.

Self Test

1. Stress can be defined as the psychological and physiological response to any stimuli that the individual perceives as threatening.

   a. true   b. false

2. Disturbing or upsetting feelings such as the ending of a relationship are _____ stressors.

   a. physical
   b. cataclysmic
   c. emotional
   d. none of these

3. Dr. Hans Selye is best known for his work with

   a. mental health and schizophrenia.
   b. stress and the general adaptation syndrome.
   c. transcendental meditation (TM).
   d. all of these

4. The alarm reaction, resistance phase, and exhaustion describe

    a. the manic-depressive syndrome.
    b. hypertension.
    c. the general adaptation syndrome.
    d. psychosocial stressors.

5. Epinephrine or adrenaline and adrenocorticotropic hormone (ACTH) are the hormones in the general adaptation syndrome.

    a. true   b. false

6. The physiologic response to stress is characterized by

    a. increased blood pressure, heart rate, and respiration.
    b. decreased salivation, dry mouth, dilated pupils, and decreased blood supply to the skin.
    c. decreased pulse, decreased vision, and increased blood pressure.
    d. a and b only

7. Many people turn to alcohol, tobacco, and other drugs in an attempt to relieve stress.

    a. true   b. false

8. Stress has very little effect on physical illness.

    a. true   b. false

9. Stress-related physical conditions are thought to include

    a. hypertension.
    b. diabetes.
    c. peptic ulcers.
    d. all of these

10. Occupational or job-related stress is an increasingly common complaint in the U.S. today.

    a. true   b. false

11. Goal clarification, time management, and good health habits are steps in

    a. transcendental meditation.
    b. risk management.
    c. stress management.
    d. general adaptation syndrome.

12. Relaxation exercises are of little use in stress management.

    a. true   b. false

13. Stress may be examined in terms of subjective or internal responses, external events that happen to us, and the non-specific response of the body.

    a. true   b. false

14. When we are under stress, we frequently experience

    a. cold hands.
    b. pounding heart.
    c. inner tightness.
    d. all of these

15. Having a Type B personality puts an individual at higher risk for coronary problems.

    a. true   b. false

16. While it cannot be said that stress causes a heart attack, stress is almost surely related to higher risk.

    a. true   b. false

17. Support systems do not make much difference in a person's ability to cope with stress.

    a. true   b. false

18. All of these are useful in coping with stress *except*

    a. biofeedback.
    b. exercise.
    c. competition.
    d. meditation.

19. Most diseases that kill Americans are still infectious in nature rather than chronic or stress related.

    a. true   b. false

20. The physiologic response to stress is always the same.

    a. true   b. false

Answer Key

1. a (p. 30)
2. c (p. 30)
3. b (p. 33)
4. c (p. 33)
5. a (p. 36)
6. d (p. 36, TV)
7. a (p. 40)
8. b (p. 41)
9. d (pp. 42, 43)
10. a (p. 44)
11. c (pp. 45-48)
12. b (pp. 45-46)
13. a (TV)
14. d (TV)
15. b (TV)
16. a (TV)
17. b (TV)
18. c (TV)
19. b (TV)
20. a (TV)

LESSON 3   Depression...More Than Just The Blues

Simplification of outward life is not enough.   It is merely the outside.   But I am starting with the outside.   I am looking at the outside of a shell, the outside of my life -- the shell.   The complete answer is not to be found on the outside, in an outward mode of living.   This is only a technique, a road to grace.   The final answer, I know, is always inside.   But the outside can give a clue, can help one find the inward answer.   One is free, like the hermit crab, to change one's shell.

Anne Morrow Lindbergh, *Gift from the Sea*

Learning Objectives

Knowledge

Upon successful completion of all assignments in this lesson, you should be able to

1. Identify two basic dimensions of the human mind and explain how they have an impact on each other and on health.

2. Describe six physiological responses that are linked to the emotions.

3. Explain how emotional responses are learned and how people can deal with their negative emotional status to achieve emotional health.

4. Name and describe several types of nonpsychotic disorders and psychotic disorders.

5. Distinguish between the two main components of intellect and describe the activities for which they serve as a foundation.

6. Explain how self-concept, different types of therapy, and individual attention can help people develop a healthy self-image and work on mental health problems.

7. Distinguish between mild depression and clinical depression.

8. Analyze the theories of clinical depression.

9. Describe the symptoms of clinical depression.

10. Explain the commonly used treatments for depression and other emotional illnesses.

Attitude

1. Accept the role that you play in maintaining your own mental health.

2. Be able to analyze your own behavior and feelings to detect early signs of depression or other emotional difficulties.

Overview

Fortunately, we have come a long way from thinking of people with emotional problems as being "possessed by demons." Emotional problems run the gamut from minor depression (the blues) and mild anxiety (butterflies in the stomach) to very serious mental illness. This lesson will discuss those aspects that fit together to determine emotional health. You will also learn ways in which we cope with conflict and feelings, and signs that warn us that we need professional help.

It is important to view mental health in terms of your life goals, your ability to cope with life, and your relationships with other people. Obviously you are not at your best all the time. You have off times, but for the most part you should feel good about yourself, excited about life, and able to interact with those around you in a positive manner. If this is not the case, examine what is happening in your life and consider getting professional counseling.

There are many theories seeking to define how we become who we are. Most of the current theories agree that heredity, physical health, and social interaction play important roles in determining mental health. Sigmund Freud, the "Father of Psychiatry," set down the original theories against which most modern theories are compared. Later Abraham Maslow developed a theory of personality development that responded to the five basic human needs. Maslow's theory demonstrates that maintaining positive mental health is a process that continues throughout life.

All psychological theories examine ways in which individuals handle conflicts, emotions, and feelings. We all have to deal with these behaviors and we all, at times, use defense mechanisms instead of solving the problems. The key to positive mental health lies in being able to recognize these defense mechanisms instead of confusing them with real solutions to life's problems.

Everyone experiences five basic emotions: love, elation, anger, fear, and sorrow. The way in which you deal with these emotions determines to a great extent the quality of your life. Problems with depression, anxiety, and relationships frequently result from difficulties in coping with strong emotions.

Depression is one of the major emotional problems. One out of every seven Americans suffers from clinical depression, depression so severe it requires treatment. Mild cases of the "blahs" aside, depression's warning symptoms include prolonged feelings of emptiness or sadness, sleep disturbances, appetite changes, decreased energy, fatigue, sexual difficulties, or problems with decision making. Lasting episodes of these symptoms signal the need for professional help.

Most mental health problems can be treated with success using a combination of medication and counseling or psychotherapy. It is unfortunate that many suffer unnecessarily because they don't seek treatment. Failure to get help may result from not recognizing symptoms or being embarrassed about having emotional problems, as well as some other reasons. However, an individual suffering from mental health problems who does not get help is deprived of the enjoyment of a happy, fulfilling life.

If you recognize signs of problems in yourself or someone else, get professional help or encourage that person to do the same. If you take only one concept from this lesson, let it be an appreciation of the key role mental health plays in our lives. Another important concept is to develop a concern and understanding for those who don't enjoy a positive state of mental health.

Study Assignments

Textbook - Chapter 3, "Emotional Health And Intellectual Well-Being," pp. 55-83

TV - Program 3, "Depression...More Than Just The Blues"

Complete Self-Assessment, "Assessing Your Self-Esteem," on pp. 74-75 in the text.

Key Terms

psychosomatic disease (p. 56)
central nervous system (CNS) (p. 56)
peripheral nervous system (PNS) (p. 56)
somatic nervous system (SNS) (p. 57)
autonomic nervous system (ANS) (p. 57)
electroencephalogram (EEG) (p. 59)
generalization (p. 60)
defense mechanism (p. 64)
repression (p. 64)
rationalization (p. 64)
denial (p. 64)
projection (p. 64)
psychic contactlessness (p. 64)
depersonalization (p. 64)
sublimation (p. 64)
nonpsychotic disorder (p. 65)
adjustment disorder (p. 67)
anxiety disorder (p. 67)
phobia (p. 67)
panic disorder (p. 67)
personality disorder (p. 68)
schizoid personality disorder (p. 68)
narcissistic personality disorder (p. 68)
antisocial personality disorder (p. 68)
somatoform disorder (p. 69)
hypochondriasis (p. 69)
psychotic disorder (p. 69)
affective disorder (p. 69)
bipolar disorder (p. 70)
mania (p. 70)
schizophrenia (p. 70)
intellect (p. 71)
conditional response theory (p. 71)

classical conditioning theory (p. 71)
operant conditioning theory (p. 71)
social learning theory (p. 72)
self-concept (p. 76)
self-esteem (p. 76)
behavior therapy (p. 76)
organic therapy (p. 78)
electroconvulsive therapy (ECT) (p. 78)
psychosurgery (p. 78)
depression (TV)
mild/non-endogenous depression (TV)
clinical/technical/endogenous depression (TV)

Text Focus Questions

1. How do emotion and intellect affect health?

2. How does the body respond physiologically to emotion?

3. What is the relationship of homeostasis to successful coping?

4. Name and describe the most commonly used defense mechanisms.

5. What characteristics describe emotionally healthy people?

6. What are the general approaches and attitudes of society toward people with serious mental illness today? How are these similar to or different from the approach and attitude in the past?

7. What are some useful measures in problem solving and decision making?

8. What effect do those aspects of personality that we consider positive or negative have on our self-concept, self-esteem, and self-efficacy?

9. Discuss the advantages and disadvantages of different types of psychotherapeutic interventions.

TV Focus Questions

1. Distinguish between mild and clinical depression.

2. Describe the common symptoms of depression.

3. Name the three major causes of depression.

4. What is a bipolar mental disturbance?

5. How is depression treated?

6. Why is childhood depression important?

Optional Strengthening Exercises

1. Visit a community mental health resource, such as a crisis intervention service or a self-help group. Become familiar with the role such resources play in a community.

2. Keep a journal for a week, describing the ups and downs of your emotional state. Consider the situations that affected your emotional state, what actions you took, and what the results were.

Self Test

1. The affective dimension allows people to experience a wide range of feelings such as love, anger, sadness, and hope.

   a. true   b. false

2. The intellect is important but plays only a small role in mental health.

   a. true   b. false

3. The central nervous system includes

   a. all the nerves in the body.
   b. regulation of all functions of the body.
   c. the brain and spinal cord.
   d. a and b
   e. b and c

4. All of the following are useful techniques for dealing with anger *except*

   a. practicing stress management techniques.
   b. trying to reduce competitive feelings.
   c. ventilating by yelling at the adversary.
   d. figuring out what is frustrating you and doing something about it.

5. Anxiety is characterized by feelings of fear, helplessness, and things being out of control.

   a. true   b. false

6. Defense mechanisms are mental processes that indicate serious illness.

   a. true   b. false

7. A person suffering from a nonpsychotic disorder displays the following characteristics *except*

   a. recognizing and being disturbed by the symptoms.
   b. being aware of how distressing the behavior is.
   c. being out of touch with his or her surroundings.
   d. being anxious about the situation.

8. Psychotic disorders are among the most serious mental problems.

   a. true   b. false

9. The only difference between mild depression and clinical depression is the severity of the symptoms.

   a. true   b. false

10. The onset of clinical depression often follows a loss or serious illness.

    a. true   b. false

11. Recurrence of medically treated depression is quite rare.

    a. true   b. false

12. Major symptoms of depression include

    a. decreased energy, decreased appetite, and sleep change.
    b. sexual dysfunction, fatigue, and changing mood.
    c. none of these
    d. all of these

13. The relationship of a depressed parent and his/her child frequently increases the chance of the child's experiencing depression.

    a. true   b. false

14. Suicide is a risk for the depressed individual.

    a. true   b. false

15. Optimum results can be obtained by treating depression with drugs.

    a. true   b. false

16. People with schizophrenia

    a. have thought disturbances.
    b. fail to achieve expected social development.
    c. display a lack of initiative, interests, and energy.
    d. all of the above

17. Self-esteem is

    a. a person's feeling of worth and dignity.
    b. not very important to mental health.
    c. virtually unrelated to self-concept and self-efficacy.
    d. easily changed.

18. Crisis intervention services are designed to help people deal with difficult career decision problems.

    a. true   b. false

19. College counseling centers and health centers can offer students help in coping with emotional problems.

    a. true   b. false

Answer Key

1. a (text, pp. 55-56)
2. b (text, p. 56)
3. e (text, p. 56)
4. c (text, p. 61)
5. a (text, p. 63)
6. b (text, p. 64)
7. c (text, p. 66)
8. a (text, p. 69)
9. b (TV)
10. a (TV)
11. b (TV)
12. d (TV)
13. a (TV)
14. a (TV)
15. b (TV)
16. d (text, pp. 70-71)
17. a (text, p. 76)
18. b (text, p. 80)
19. a (text, p. 81)

LESSON 4   Exercise: Shaping Up

You will begin to touch heaven, Jonathan, in the moment that you touch perfect speed. And that isn't flying a thousand miles an hour, or a million, or flying at the speed of light. Because any number is a limit, and perfection doesn't have limits. Perfect speed, my son, is being there.

Richard Bach, *Jonathan Livingston Seagull*

Learning Objectives

Knowledge

Upon successful completion of all assignments in this lesson, you should be able to

1. Differentiate between activity and exercise and discuss the benefits and dangers of exercise.

2. Define 11 different components of fitness, distinguishing between those that are skill related and those that are health related.

3. Explore the benefits of flexibility, strength, endurance, and cardiovascular fitness, indicating which types of exercises promote each one.

4. Name and discuss four general principles that should underlie every exercise program.

5. Discuss the health benefits of exercise for children.

6. Explain heart rate monitoring.

7. List and explain the precautions one should take before beginning an exercise program.

Attitude

1. Explain the concept of physical fitness as a personal responsibility.

2. Analyze your own reasons for being or for not being involved in a regular exercise program.

Overview

When Dr. Joe Mitchell said, "Joggers don't live longer, it just seems so," he was describing one of the many reasons why people exercise regularly. Those who exercise regularly feel better, look better, and are generally healthier than people who don't.

Exercise will benefit you, no matter what your age. You can start an exercise program at any time. It is not necessary to build great muscles or run a marathon in order to be in good shape. Fitness is measured by having the energy and ability to do the things you want to and to meet the demands placed upon you. Most people can start a walking program even if they can't jog, swim, or do more strenuous exercise. The good news is that walking is an excellent aerobic exercise that will condition the heart, lungs, and muscles -- it just takes a little longer than the more strenuous exercises.

Using good judgment in an exercise program is important. If you have been inactive for several years, are over 30 years old, or suffer from a chronic illness, examination by a physician is very important. Your physician can order tests that will help ensure that you are ready for an exercise program.

People usually feel improvement in their condition within a month or so of beginning an aerobic exercise program. That improvement will continue. Conversely, conditioning can be lost in only a few weeks or months if you stop the exercise program.

So, get a checkup, put on those running shoes, and hit the road! If you think you might need a little extra motivation and help, enroll in a class at a college near you or join a good fitness club.

Study Assignments

Textbook - Chapter 4, "Activity, Exercise, And Physical Fitness," pp. 85-100

TV - Program 4, "Exercise -- Shaping Up"

Complete Self-Assessment, "How Fit Are You," on pp. 98-99 in the text.

Key Terms

physical activity (p. 87)
physical exercise (p. 87)
amenorrhea (p. 90)
agility (p. 90)
balance (p. 90)
coordination (p. 90)
power (p. 90)
reaction time (p. 90)
speed (p. 90)
flexibility (p. 90, TV)
muscular strength (p. 90, TV)
muscular endurance (p. 90, TV)

cardiovascular fitness (p. 90)
body leanness (p. 91)
atrophy (p. 93)
isokinetic (p. 94)
isotonic (p. 94, TV)
isometric (p. 94, TV)
vital capacity (p. 95)
maximum breathing capacity (p. 95)
aerobic exercise (p. 96, TV)
anaerobic exercise (p. 97, TV)
specificity (p. 97)
overload (p. 97)
progression (p. 100)
regularity (p. 100)
anaerobic (TV)
warm-up (TV)
cool-down (TV)
ballistic (TV)
duration (TV)
frequency (TV)
target heart rate (TV)
stroke volume (TV)
static (TV)
dynamic (TV)
cardiovascular endurance (TV)

Text Focus Questions

1. What are the major and related benefits of regular exercise?

2. Compare physical activity and physical exercise.

3. How can regular physical exercise improve emotional well-being?

4. What are the skill-related components and the health-related components of physical fitness? Explain each component.

5. What are the important steps to be considered in developing each aspect of health-related fitness?

6. What are the four basic principles of exercise? Explain the importance of each.

TV Focus Questions

1. What are the health benefits of exercise for children and adults?

2. What must be done to gain the benefits from exercise?

3. What are the effects of exercise on the major risk factors of heart disease?

4. What is heart rate monitoring? How is it done?

5. What are the points that should be considered before embarking on an exercise program?

6. Describe the best kind of exercise.

Optional Strengthening Exercises

1. Design an exercise program that would promote overall fitness.

2. Evaluate your physical activity, keeping an activity diary/log for one week. List the activities and note the intensity and duration for each. How would you rate your activity level?

Self Test

1. The physically fit person is able to withstand greater physical and emotional stress than the person who is not fit.

   a. true   b. false

2. Although all the body systems are stimulated with regular exercise, the _____ and _____ systems receive the greatest benefit.

   a. neurological, skeletal
   b. cardiovascular, respiratory
   c. neurological, cardiovascular
   d. respiratory, skeletal

3. Other people, particularly experts, should make the decisions about exercise for us.

   a. true   b. false

4. Physical exercise includes

   a. household tasks.
   b. walking across the parking lot.
   c. jogging two miles four times a week.
   d. all of these

5. The ability to exercise the whole body for long periods and have the circulatory system supply the fuel that keeps the body going is

   a. flexibility.
   b. cardiovascular fitness.
   c. muscular endurance.
   d. muscular strength.

6. Agility, balance, power, and speed are considered _____ components of physical fitness.

    a. essential
    b. health-related
    c. skill-related
    d. none of these

7. Flexibility is rarely necessary in our normal day's activities.

    a. true   b. false

8. If muscle tissue is not used, it will atrophy or grow smaller.

    a. true   b. false

9. _____ exercise is the least useful method for building muscle strength and endurance.

    a. Isokinetic
    b. Isotonic
    c. Nautilus
    d. Isometric

10. _____ exercise is the most useful method for developing cardiovascular fitness.

    a. Aerobic
    b. Anaerobic
    c. Isokinetic
    d. Isotonic

11. The _____ portion of an exercise session stretches the muscles and gets the body ready for the exercise activity.

   a. cool-down
   b. aerobic
   c. warm-up
   d. isometric

12. _____ is the principle that to develop a component of fitness, one must work on that particular component.

   a. Overload
   b. Specificity
   c. Progression
   d. Regularity

13. _____ is the principle that exercise needs to be done frequently enough, with enough intensity, and for a sufficient period of time.

   a. Progression
   b. Specificity
   c. Fitness
   d. Regularity

14. To be effective, the _____ of an exercise program should be the equivalent of a 15-minute/three times per week session.

   a. frequency
   b. intensity
   c. duration
   d. specificity

15. Most people under 50 can start an exercise program of any intensity they wish without any preliminary checkups.

    a. true   b. false

16. Exercise has become so popular that about half of the population exercise every day.

    a. true   b. false

17. Exercise is valuable in that it

    a. decreases fatigue.
    b. increases energy.
    c. improves shape.
    d. all of these

18. Some good aerobic exercises are

    a. walking.
    b. jogging.
    c. bicycling.
    d. golfing.
    e. swimming.
    f. all except d

19. Static exercises are good for everyone.

    a. true   b. false

20. Generally, during an aerobic exercise session the heart should work at 60% to 80% of its maximum capacity.

    a. true   b. false

Answer Key

1. a (p. 85)
2. b (TV)
3. b (p. 86)
4. c (p. 87)
5. b (p. 90)
6. c (p. 90)
7. b (p. 92)
8. a (p. 93)
9. d (p. 94)
10. a (p. 96)
11. c (p. 96)
12. b (p. 97)
13. d (p. 100)
14. a (TV)
15. b (TV)
16. a (TV)
17. d (TV)
18. f (TV)
19. b (TV)
20. a (TV)

LESSON 5   Sports Injuries

The next night from the Flock came Kirk Maynard Gull, wobbling across the sand, dragging his left wing, to collapse at Jonathan's feet. "Help me," he said very quietly, speaking in the way that the dying speak. "I want to fly more than anything else in the world"...

"Come along then," said Jonathan, "Climb with me away from the ground, and we'll begin."

"You don't understand. My wing. I can't move my wing."

"Maynard Gull, you have the freedom to be yourself, your true self, here and now, and nothing can stand in your way. It is the Law of the Great Gull, the Law that is."

"I say you are free!"

As simply and as quickly as that, Kirk Maynard Gull spread his wings, effortlessly, and lifted into the dark night air. The Flock was roused from sleep by his cry, as loud as he could scream it, from five hundred feet up: "I can fly! Listen! I CAN FLY!"

Richard Bach, *Jonathan Livingston Seagull*

Learning Objectives

Knowledge

Upon successful completion of all assignments in this lesson, you should be able to

1. Describe important stages in developing a sound exercise plan to meet personal goals.

2. Explain why an exercise plan should become a permanent part of a person's weekly routine, adapted throughout the person's life span.

3. Describe some aspects that should be considered before joining a health club.

4. Explain the Overuse-Overstress Syndrome.

5. Discuss the common exercise injuries.

6. List the first-aid procedures for exercise (sports) injuries.

7. Describe the precautions that should be taken to prevent exercise-related injuries.

8. Discuss prevention of injuries in adolescent sports.

9. Explain pain as a key to severity of injury in exercise.

10. List the guidelines that should be followed for an exercise program.

Attitude

1. Analyze your own exercise program or plans for one. Discuss the injury-preventing components.

Overview

Choosing the proper exercises and following the guidelines for preventing injury are the most important factors in an exercise program. Almost everyone can do something to improve his or her level of fitness. If you don't believe this, take a look at the participants in senior citizens' exercise programs and cardiac rehabilitation programs.

Some tips for selecting the program that is right for you include choosing something you like to do (or think you will enjoy); choosing something you are likely to be able to do most of your life; making certain that whatever else you do, you include aerobic exercise in your program; practicing adequate warm-up and cool-down in each session. Proper equipment also is extremely important. (Note: selecting jogging shoes is not an area to cut cost at expense of quality.)

If you have been sedentary for several years or are over 30 years old, it is wise to consult your family physician before beginning a program. Your fitness instructor also can help you design a program that will get you in shape while minimizing your risks of injury. Remember, fitness takes time no matter who you are. Getting out and running fast and far the first time is *not* the answer. Sports injuries are much easier to prevent than they are to cure. No matter what exercise program you begin, follow these guidelines for maximum fitness with minimum risk of injury:

1. Warm up for 5 to 10 minutes.
2. Do stretching exercises.

3. Develop your program for three to four times per week for 25 to 30 minutes of exercise per session. Build your working heart rate to 130-140 beats per minute.
4. Progress slowly.
5. Don't overstress your body.
6. Cool down.
7. "Listen" when your body complains.
8. Make this the year you get physically fit!

Study Assignments

Textbook - Chapter 4, "Activity, Exercise, And Physical Fitness," pp. 101-109

TV - Program 5, "Sports Injuries"

Key Terms

Overuse-Overstress Syndrome (TV)
endomorphine (TV)
shin splints (TV)

Text Focus Questions

1. What are the steps to be taken to develop an exercise plan? Discuss each step.

2. Why is it important to get medical approval before beginning an exercise program?

3. How does one choose a good health club?

4. What are some tips that will help you sustain your fitness program?

TV Focus Questions

1. What is the Overuse-Overstress Syndrome?

2. What are some of the other common exercise (sports) injuries and how are they treated?

3. What basic first-aid measures are used for exercise (sports) injuries?

4. What steps should be taken to prevent exercise (sports) injuries in an exercise program?

5. Why are adolescents more prone to sports injuries? How can these risks be reduced?

6. How do pain levels associated with exercise give clues to the severity of the problem?

7. What are the guidelines that should be followed to reduce the risk of injury in an exercise program?

Optional Strengthening Exercises

1. Observe participants in an exercise session and note whether they follow the guidelines for injury prevention. Does their exercise program contain the warm-up and cool-down components? What other aspects of the session are noteworthy? Evaluate the session.

2. Follow the above procedures to evaluate an adolescent's sports activity.

Self Test

1. The first step in developing an exercise plan is

    a. deciding where and when to exercise.
    b. assessing fitness needs.
    c. evaluating general fitness goals.
    d. choosing a health club.

2. Assessing one's fitness needs is of little importance in the overall exercise plan.

    a. true   b. false

3. Walking briskly for at least three hours per week can improve health significantly.

    a. true   b. false

4. For most people _____ of continuous aerobic activity per session is considered optimal.

    a. 5-10 minutes
    b. 10-20 minutes
    c. 20-60 minutes
    d. at least 60 minutes

5. It is a good idea to obtain medical clearance before beginning a fitness program.

    a. true   b. false

6. Weather is of little significance in an exercise schedule.

    a. true   b. false

7. Setting realistic goals is helpful in sustaining an exercise program.

    a. true   b. false

8. Once a person is in good physical condition, an occasional exercise session will maintain the desired level of fitness.

    a. true   b. false

9. The Overuse-Overstress Syndrome is a result of

    a.   constant, repetitive injury.
    b.   acute injury.
    c.   reinjuring of an old injury.
    d.   none of these

10. The _____ is the most commonly injured part of the body during regular exercise.

    a.   ankle
    b.   hip
    c.   shin
    d.   knee

11. A common minor injury to people beginning exercise programs, characterized by pain in the front of the leg below the knee, is

    a.   fracture of the fibula.
    b.   torn cartilage in the knee.
    c.   shin splints.
    d.   hip dysplasia.

12. The steps in first aid for minor sports injuries (in the proper order) are

    a. anti-inflammatory drugs (such as aspirin), ice, strength development, stretching.
    b. ice, anti-inflammatory drugs (such as aspirin), stretching, strength development.
    c. stretching, ice, anti-inflammatory drugs (such as aspirin), strength building.
    d. ice, stretching, anti-inflammatory drugs (such as aspirin), strength building.

13. One of the keys to prevent sports injuries is to match players' sizes in contact sports.

    a. true   b. false

14. The keys to preventing injuries in exercise programs consist of

    a. flexibility and strength development.
    b. cardiovascular conditioning and good reflexes.
    c. choosing sports that fit your genetic capability, age, and social and economic level.
    d. all of these

15. Pain during exercise that lowers performance level doesn't necessarily need to be checked by a physician. Frequently it will work itself out.

    a. true   b. false

16. It can be said that the warm-up and stretching portion of an exercise program is the most important part.

    a. true   b. false

Answer Key

1. c (p. 101)
2. b (p. 101)
3. a (p. 103)
4. c (p. 103)
5. a (p. 104)
6. b (p. 105)
7. a (p. 106)
8. b (p. 107)
9. a (TV)
10. d (TV)
11. c (TV)
12. b (TV)
13. a (TV)
14. d (TV)
15. b (TV)
16. a (TV)

LESSON 6   Nutrition: Eating To Live Or Living To Eat

"Everything I like is illegal, immoral, or fattening."

Unknown

Learning Objectives

Knowledge

Upon successful completion of all assignments in this lesson, you should be able to

1. Define nutrition and explain the importance of diet and proper nutrition to health.

2. List seven different classes of components in food, including fiber and water, specifying foods that are good sources for each component.

3. Explain some of the important functions of the major components and nutrients in food.

4. Describe the two classic strategies for determining a proper diet and discuss the drawbacks of each one.

5. Discuss the basic principles of a positive food strategy and analyze and plan a daily diet based on these principles.

6. Explain some of the strategies for buying and preparing food that can help ensure that one eats a nutritious diet.

7. Identify five universal principles that can provide guidance for anyone who wishes to eat healthily in today's world.

8. Name the major sources of cholesterol in the diet and analyze the effects of cholesterol on the body.

9. Compare the effects of HDL and LDL cholesterol on the body.

10. Analyze diet patterns that will help decrease the risk of heart disease.

11. Discuss the sources of salt and the desired amounts for good nutrition.

12. Describe the effects that too much salt has on the body.

Attitude

1. Analyze your dietary habits; pay particular attention to fats, sugar, and salt.

2. Compare your diet to recommended guidelines.

Overview

A strange dichotomy exists in America's nutrition. We are simultaneously overfed and malnourished. Most people overeat regularly, often choosing foods that are high in saturated fats, salt, and refined sugar, rather than vegetables, fruits, or broiled meat or fish. What's even worse, children eat just like adults, thus increasing their risk of nutrition-related diseases.

Americans dine in a land of plenty -- plenty of the wrong foods. Recall what you learned about the basic food groups in elementary school. Revive that knowledge and use it in planning your current dietary intake. This lesson contains technical information about nutrients and guidelines for good nutrition. It is important to know what types of foods are necessary for total nutrition and which ones should be avoided or limited.

Why not change your diet to one that is nutritionally adequate and that lowers your risk of disease? The following guidelines show you how to get started.

1. Decrease your beef and pork intake. Instead, make your "meat" selection from poultry or fish.

2. Decrease your consumption of eggs, butter, and hard cheese.

3. Decrease your intake of salt and refined sugar.

4. Avoid high-caloric snacks.

5. Increase your intake of whole grain breads and cereals.

6. Increase your intake of fruits and green, leafy vegetables.

7. Increase your intake of foods containing fiber.

8. Broil, boil, steam, or bake food -- don't fry it.

You are probably familiar with all these health tips, but do you practice them? A well-balanced diet can be just as tasty as junk food. Try eating to live instead of living to eat. With a healthier body, you will be a winner.

Study Assignments

Textbook - Chapter 5, "Diet And Nutrition," pp. 111-137

TV - Program 6, "Nutrition: Eating To Live Or Living To Eat"

Key Terms

metabolism (p. 112)
calorie (p. 112)
macronutrient (p. 112)
micronutrient (p. 112)
protein (p. 112)
enzyme (p. 112)
essential amino acid (p. 113)
complete protein (p. 113)
incomplete protein (p. 113)
glucose (p. 114)
carbohydrates (p. 114, TV)
glycogen (p. 115)
lipids (p. 115)
triglycerides (p. 115)
cholesterol (p. 115, TV)
unsaturated fat (p. 116, TV)
saturated fat (p. 116, TV)
minerals (p. 117)
calcium (p. 117)
potassium (p. 119)
sodium (p. 119, TV)
electrolytes (p. 119)
iron (p. 119)
vitamins (p. 119)
water-soluble vitamins (p. 121)
biochemical individuality (p. 121)

fat-soluble vitamins (p. 122)
fiber (roughage) (TV)
LDL cholesterol (TV)
HDL cholesterol (TV)

Text Focus Questions

1. What is nutrition? What part does metabolism play in nutrition?

2. What are the basic components of food? How is each used?

3. Name the basic four food groups. What are the drawbacks of using this plan for describing good nutrition?

4. What is the exchange system? What drawbacks does it have in helping people plan their nutritional program?

5. What are the four principles in the positive food strategy? How is this plan helpful in planning good nutrition?

6. How can stress affect nutrition?

7. How can one become a more well informed grocery shopper?

8. Describe some of the basic guidelines used in preparing nutritious low-fat, low-salt, low-sugar meals.

9. What are some of the basic principles to use in developing healthy eating habits?

TV Focus Questions

1. What are some of the troublesome trends in the present American diet?

2. What role do fats play in nutrition?

3. Compare saturated fats with polyunsaturated fats in characteristics and effects on the body.

4. Why are HDL and LDL cholesterol important to nutrition and body functions?

5. What lifestyle habits and other conditions influence HDL and LDL cholesterol?

6. What are the sources of salt in diet intake? What amount of salt is sufficient for good nutrition?

7. What are the effects of too much salt in the body?

8. Name the important dietary patterns that should be followed by most individuals.

Optional Strengthening Exercises

1. Keep a record of your dietary intake for a week. Note foods containing cholesterol and saturated fats, those high in salt, and those that contain "empty" calories (those with little nutritional value).

2. Evaluate your diet using the recommendations in your textbook or on the TV program.

Self Test

1. _____ is the amount of heat needed to raise one kilogram of water one degree Celsius and is the unit needed to measure the energy potential of food.

   a. Metabolism
   b. Macronutrient
   c. Calorie
   d. None of these

2. Enzymes are a type of protein that builds up and breaks down cellular material in the body.

   a. true   b. false

3. Meat, poultry, fish, dried beans, peas, eggs, cheese, and milk are leading sources of

   a. fat.
   b. protein.
   c. carbohydrates.
   d. Vitamin C.

4. _____ play an important role as the body's chief and most immediate source of energy.

   a. Proteins
   b. Carbohydrates
   c. Fats
   d. Vitamins

5. Table sugar is a complex carbohydrate.

   a. true   b. false

6. _____ is/are an important ingredient in the walls of every cell, contribute(s) to blood clotting and hormone synthesis, insulate(s) the body, and surround(s) vital organs.

   a. Proteins
   b. Carbohydrates
   c. Fats
   d. Fiber

7. Most of the fat eaten should be unsaturated rather than saturated.

   a. true   b. false

8. Men and women need approximately the same amount of calcium in their diet.

   a. true   b. false

9. Large doses of vitamins are needed to supplement even a well-balanced diet.

   a. true   b. false

10. _____ binds waste products with water in the colon and passes through the digestive system unchanged.

   a. Protein
   b. Fat
   c. Carbohydrate
   d. Fiber

11. Most Americans should reduce their intake of simple carbohydrates and increase their intake of complex carbohydrates.

   a. true   b. false

12. Refined sugar provides a variety of nutrients needed for good nutrition.

   a. true   b. false

13. Water is one of the less important food components.

   a. true   b. false

14. Approximately half of the daily food intake should consist of milk and meat products.

   a. true   b. false

15. The basic goal of a positive food strategy is to
   a. increase the intake of complex carbohydrates.
   b. decrease the intake of protein.
   c. limit the intake of fat.
   d. all of these

16. Fat is a concentrated high-energy nutrient that is overconsumed by Americans.

   a. true   b. false

17. Saturated fats are

    a. hard at room temperature.
    b. primarily in animal fats.
    c. linked with heart disease.
    d. all of these
    e. none of these

18. Excess cholesterol in the bloodstream can result in the formation of plaque on arterial walls, causing them to lose their elasticity.

    a. true   b. false

19. Practices linked to an increase in cardiovascular disease include

    a. eating half of your meals outside the home.
    b. increasing consumption of saturated fats.
    c. decreasing intake of complex carbohydrates.
    d. increasing intake of salt and refined sugar.
    e. practicing a sedentary lifestyle.
    f. all of these
    g. all except c and e
    h. d and e only

20. It would be very difficult to lower cholesterol intake to dangerous levels.

    a. true   b. false

21. A difficulty in good diet planning for the vegetarian is obtaining the needed nutrients from fewer food groups.

    a. true   b. false

22. Excessive stress over prolonged periods can cause a phenomenon known as vitamin depletion.

    a. true   b. false

23. Careful reading of labels can help the consumer buy more healthful food.

    a. true   b. false

24. Frying is one of the most nutritious ways to cook food since it adds much-needed fat to the diet.

    a. true   b. false

25. Raw fruits and vegetables have more nutritional value than well-cooked ones.

    a. true   b. false

26. General dietary habits that should be adhered to include

    a. increasing your intake of whole grains.
    b. decreasing your intake of beef and pork.
    c. decreasing your intake of eggs and butter.
    d. increasing your vegetable intake.
    e. increasing your fiber intake.
    f. decreasing your salt intake.
    g. all of these
    h. c, d, e, and f only
    i. a, b, and d only

Answer Key

1. c (p. 112)
2. a (p. 112)
3. b (p. 113, TV)
4. b (p. 114)
5. b (p. 114)
6. c (p. 115)
7. a (p. 116)
8. b (p. 119)
9. b (pp. 119, 122)
10. d (p. 122)
11. a (TV)
12. b (TV)
13. b (p. 123)
14. b (p. 124)
15. d (p. 127)
16. a (TV)
17. d (TV)
18. a (TV)
19. f (TV)
20. a (TV)
21. a (p. 129)
22. a (p. 130)
23. a (p. 133)
24. b (pp. 133, 134)
25. a (p. 136)
26. g (TV)

LESSON 7   Obesity And The Slimming Of America

"I'm not overweight, I'm undertall."

**Garfield Poster
by Jim Davis**

Learning Objectives

Knowledge

Upon successful completion of all assignments in this lesson, you should be able to

1. Describe the relationship among weight, appearance, and body composition and list some of the problems associated with unhealthy body composition.

2. Explain the different uses of fats in the human body, indicating which ones cause the most problems in regard to healthy body composition.

3. Identify and comment on at least four different techniques Americans use to control and manage appearance and body composition.

4. Characterize two approaches that underlie explanations of body composition problems and explain how to work on them.

5. Explain how people can use natural management techniques for body composition.

6. Name and describe three extreme conditions that occasionally affect body composition, indicating current ideas about their cause and treatment.

63

7. Describe the problems related to three levels of obesity: modestly obese, seriously obese, massively (morbidly) obese.

8. Compare the eating patterns of a morbidly obese individual with a person of normal weight.

9. Discuss the psychological aspects of obesity.

10. List the important principles a person attempting to lose weight should follow.

11. Describe some of the radical treatments for obesity.

12. Discuss anorexia nervosa and bulimia.

Attitude

1. Examine your own physical appearance in terms of height and weight and eating habits. Determine what category you fall into and make a decision to correct your weight if necessary.

Overview

Have you noticed how obsessed many people become with every new diet that comes along? Frankly, obesity is a major problem in our country today, and obese people are more likely to develop serious diseases as a result of their heavier bulk. However, when people of any size resort to gimmicks, fad diets, or other quick weight-loss schemes, they put themselves at major risk of developing other health problems.

A person may temporarily lose weight on any of the fad diets but will rapidly regain the weight when he or she returns to the old eating patterns. One weight-loss gimmick that includes wrapping the body to reduce weight actually draws off body fluids -- leading to an extremely dangerous situation. Some people have even died as a result of using such fad diets and/or gimmicks.

To lose weight and then keep it off necessitates a change in lifestyle and eating habits. For most, this means eating a well-balanced diet that contains fewer calories than the body is using. Increased exercise also is important in this process. Any person who is extremely overweight or who has other health problems must be under the supervision of a physician. Healthy persons who have 20 to 30 pounds to lose can do so if they know what a nutritious, low-calorie diet is and if they use good judgment when participating in an exercise program. If there is any doubt in your mind about your diet and/or exercise program, seek professional guidance.

Taking that first step is not easy, but it is so rewarding when you gradually achieve that ideal weight. Safely losing weight takes time and effort.

The principles you will learn in these lessons on nutrition and weight control are beneficial whether you are overweight, underweight, or just right. A nutritious, well-balanced diet combined with a sensible exercise program is important for everyone. Use the knowledge you'll gain in this lesson to eat healthily for life.

Study Assignments

Textbook - Chapter 6, "Weight Management And Body Composition," pp. 139-166

TV - Program 7, "Obesity And The Slimming of America"

Complete Self-Assessment, "Body Composition: A Ready Reckoner," on p. 143 in the text.

Key Terms

body composition (p. 140)
essential fat (p. 142)
storage fat (p. 142)
hydrostatic weighing method (p. 144)
bioelectrical impedance (p. 144)
skinfold measurement (p. 144)
liposuction (p. 149)
pull school (p. 151)
push school (p. 151)
short-term regulatory mechanism (p. 151)
long-term regulatory mechanism (p. 151)
setpoint theory (p. 152)
basal metabolism (p. 152)
externality theory (p. 154)
obesity (TV)
hyperplasia (TV)
hypertrophy (TV)
calorie (TV)
metabolism (TV)
anorexia nervosa (p. 160)
bulimia (p. 162)
morbidly obese (TV)

Text Focus Questions

1. What is the relationship of body composition to physical health? To emotional health? To social health?

2. Describe the nature and types of fat.

3. How can we calculate body composition?

4. List the criteria that can be used to evaluate the health and safety of diets.

5. What is the role of exercise in management of body composition?

6. How can drugs be dangerous when used in weight control?

7. What are some of the dangers of the surgery used in weight loss?

8. Compare the characteristics of some of the group weight-loss programs.

9. Contrast the pull school and the push school approaches to explaining body composition problems.

10. How can body composition be successfully controlled over the long term?

11. Compare anorexia nervosa and bulimia. What are the serious results of these conditions?

TV Focus Questions

1. What constitutes modest, serious, and massive overweight? What are the characteristics of each?

2. How are the eating patterns of the morbidly obese individual different from those of a normal person?

3. What are some of the psychological problems associated with overweight?

4. Why is it more difficult for the person with a hyperplasia condition to lose weight than one with hypertrophy to lose weight?

5. What are some of the important principles that can help an individual trying to lose weight?

6. What are some of the radical approaches to treating the massively obese person? When are these used?

7. What are the three components of a good weight-loss program?

Optional Strengthening Exercise

1. Conduct your own observational exercise concerning degrees of obesity using the following method:

   a. Observe approximately 100 people at a high traffic area such as the airport, shopping mall, department store, or college campus.

   b. Estimate the number who fall into the categories of normal weight, modestly overweight, seriously overweight, and massively overweight.

   c. At home calculate the percentage falling into each category. Note whether your calculations were similar to the national percentages mentioned in the TV program.

   d. If not, do you have any ideas as to why (i.e., age factors, location of the observation experiment, etc.)?

   e. Did anything in your observations surprise you? Did you notice any of the obesity-related symptoms in your group? Did you have the opportunity to see the eating patterns of any of the people you observed? If so, what did you notice?

Self Test

1. Approximately _____ percent of the U.S. population is overweight.

    a. 10-15
    b. 25-30
    c. 50-60
    d. none of the above

2. The most commonly observed problems associated with being overweight include

    a. fatigue and lack of energy.
    b. shortness of breath.
    c. hypertension and heart problems.
    d. all of these

3. Some of the diseases commonly linked with obesity are

    a. heart disease.
    b. hypertension.
    c. diabetes.
    d. gallbladder disease.
    e. all of these

4. There is little relationship between body composition and emotional health.

    a. true   b. false

5. Women need significantly less essential fat than do men.

    a. true   b. false

6. _____ is fat deposited under the skin and around the internal organs to protect them.

    a. Cell wall fat
    b. Essential fat
    c. Fatty acid
    d. Storage fat

7. The only completely accurate means for measuring body composition is hydrostatic weighing.

    a. true   b. false

8. A weight loss of _____ per week is considered realistic and healthy.

    a. no more than one pound
    b. one to two pounds
    c. three to five pounds
    d. at least five pounds

9. Hyperplasia results in an exceptionally large number of fat cells, making weight loss more difficult.

    a. true   b. false

10. Extremely low-calorie, low-carbohydrate, low-protein diets can be quite dangerous.

    a. true   b. false

11. One pound of body weight is equal to approximately _____ calories. Therefore, if you store this many calories, you gain a pound, but if you utilize this many calories without replacing them, you'll lose a pound.

    a. 2000
    b. 2500
    c. 3000
    d. 3500
    e. more than 4000

12. When one is dieting, he or she should refrain from exercising because exercise increases the appetite.

    a. true   b. false

13. The pull school believes weight problems are greatly influenced by physiological factors, but the push school sees them as more a result of psychological or social factors.

    a. true   b. false

14. The basic principle of weight regulation is the energy-balance equation:

    a. change in energy store = energy intake + energy expenditure
    b. change in energy store = energy intake x energy expenditure
    c. change in energy store = energy intake - energy expenditure
    d. change in energy store = energy intake divided by energy expenditure

15. Fad diets and weight-loss gimmicks rarely work and indeed can be very dangerous.

    a. true   b. false

16. The life-threatening eating disorder characterized by chronic self-starvation resulting from a personal feeling of being too fat is

    a. bulimia.
    b. obesity.
    c. adipose.
    d. anorexia nervosa.

17. The eating disorder characterized by a pattern of eating binges, followed by self-induced vomiting or consumption of laxatives, is known as bulimia.

    a. true   b. false

18. It is common to _____ weight as we grow older.

    a. lose
    b. gain

19. Unlike a person of normal weight, a morbidly obese person tends to eat when hungry.

    a. true   b. false

20. Obesity is characterized by

    a. the person consuming more calories than needed.
    b. the person consuming fewer calories than needed.
    c. the person's body not efficiently storing calories.
    d. the person's body is very efficiently storing calories.
    e. a and c
    f. a and d
    g. b and d

21. All of these factors will help you lose weight sensibly, *except*

    a. decreasing the amount of food eaten.
    b. increasing your activities.
    c. eating slowly and chewing food thoroughly.
    d. eating low-calorie foods.
    e. trying a quick weight-loss fad diet.

22. All of these are radical methods for controlling obesity *except*

    a. a well-balanced diet.
    b. an Ilial bypass.
    c. a protein formula.
    d. a rice diet.

Answer Key

1. b (TV)
2. a (TV)
3. e (p. 140, TV)
4. b (p. 141)
5. b (p. 142)
6. d (p. 142)
7. b (p. 144)
8. b (p. 146)
9. a (TV)
10. a (p. 146)
11. d (TV)
12. b (p. 148)
13. a (p. 151)
14. c (p. 155)
15. a (TV)
16. d (p. 160)
17. a (p. 162)
18. b (TV)
19. b (TV)
20. f (TV)
21. e (TV)
22. a (TV)

LESSON 8   Adolescent Anxiety

The pure relationship, how beautiful it is! How easily it is damaged, or weighed down with irrelevancies -- not even irrelevancies, just life itself, the accumulations of life and of time. For the first part of every relationship is pure, whether it be friend or lover, husband or child. It is pure, simple and unencumbered. It is like the artist's vision before he has to discipline it into form, or like the flower of love before it has ripened into the firm but heavy fruit of responsibility. Two people listening to each other, two shells meeting each other, making one world between them. There are no others in the perfect unity of that instant, no other people or things or interests. It is free of ties or claims, unburdened by responsibilities, by worry about the future or debts to the past.

Anne Morrow Lindbergh, *Gifts from the Sea*

Learning Objectives

Knowledge

Upon successful completion of all assignments in this lesson, you should be able to

1. Explain the importance of intimate relationships, identify some barriers to forming intimate relationships, and discuss ways to overcome these barriers.

2. Identify and describe alternatives to marriage.

3. Explain why divorce is on the increase and discuss some of its potential effects on a couple and their children.

4. Discuss how the role of parenthood has changed in recent years and describe how parents can foster healthy physical, emotional, intellectual, social, and spiritual development in their children.

5. Identify some of the factors associated with the incidence of domestic violence and describe various characteristics of battering by abusive parents.

6. Discuss the nature of child abuse in the United States today and explain the effects of abuse on children.

7. Identify the most common conflicts between adolescents and their parents.

8. Explain the development task of adolescence.

9. Discuss tasks parents face in allowing their adolescents to mature.

Attitude

1. If you are a parent or an adult, describe methods you could use for improving communication with your adolescent. If you are an adolescent, describe methods you could use to improve communications with your parent.

2. Analyze your own feelings toward mate selection and marriage or living together by explaining your attitudes.

Overview

All our lives we are engaged in relationships of some kind. Of these, the most intense and often difficult are the "romantic love" and the parental/adolescent relationships. There are many reasons why difficulties occur with these two types of relationships. However, communication (or lack of communication) is the most important one.

In this lesson you will learn a great deal about developing and maintaining good relationships. You may also recognize some of the issues that have caused problems in relationships you have had or are now engaged in. Volumes have been written about relationships, and many writers have earned large amounts of money discussing the problems of relationships. The basic tenets are fairly simple; however, believing that these tenets are important and following them can be difficult.

The first serious conflicts within relationships usually occur in adolescence, a time of great intensity and turmoil. The teenager must learn independence, begin to separate from parents, and learn to cope in an adult world. Parents must allow this development and serve as role models. This is easy to explain, but the process of carrying it through can be incredibly complex. Fortunately, most teens (and their parents) get through this period successfully. However, the next stage of their lives, romantic love, also is full of crisis.

Developing a good romantic relationship, choosing the right mate, and maintaining a healthy relationship are challenging to say the least. The successful outcome of all this work is the most satisfying relationship an individual can experience -- a good marriage. Of course marriage is not the only normal lifestyle, but a marriage is still the most common. Marriages are not "made in heaven," and healthy relationships require effort and commitment on a daily basis.

This lesson is important to adolescents, parents, and adults searching for the "best" possible relationships in their lives.

Study Assignments

Textbook - Chapter 7, "Marriage, Family, And Other Intimate Relationships," pp. 169-195

TV - Program 8, "Adolescent Anxiety"

Complete Self-Assessment, "Your Attitudes About Household Tasks," on p. 176 in the text.

Key Term

cohabitation (p. 175)

Text Focus Questions

1. Why do people marry? What are some alternatives to marriage?

2. How should one choose a suitable mate? What are some of the most important tasks involved in sustaining a relationship?

3. How has the incidence of divorce changed through the years? Discuss the effect of divorce on the family.

4. What are some of the reasons for having children today?

5. In what ways are parents responsible for the various aspects of their children's development?

6. Why and how has the role of the traditional full-time mother changed? The role of the father?

7. What things should the parents consider when selecting child care alternatives?

8. Discuss some of the problems encountered in child rearing, including single parenthood.

9. Why do family members abuse and commit violent acts against each other?

10. Why do people abuse their children? What are some potential solutions to this problem?

11. What are some of the most common problems in intimate relationships?

TV Focus Questions

1. How is adolescence a rehearsal for adulthood?

2. Discuss the important developmental task(s) of adolescence.

3. What is a parent's role in the adolescent's development?

4. Discuss some of the common issues that the adolescent is facing.

5. What is the one most critical aspect of the relationship between adolescents and their parents?

6. What are some of the symptoms of communication problems between parents and adolescents?

7. What are some of the important issues surrounding sexual relationships that the adolescent must learn?

8. List some of the important things that the adolescent must learn in order to be ready for adulthood.

Optional Strengthening Exercises

1. Interview some adolescents concerning their feelings about the most difficult experiences they are encountering, the decisions they have to make, the kind of relationships that are important to them, etc.

2. Interview some of your married friends and some who are living in alternative lifestyles. Ask them about their relationships: strengths, difficulties, etc.

3. Visit a crisis center/hot line or similar agency and find out the most common relationship problems they deal with and methods they use to help in these situations.

Self Test

1. The marriage rate has _____ since 1950.

    a. increased slightly
    b. increased significantly
    c. decreased slightly
    d. decreased dramatically

2. Teenage dating prepares the adolescent for

    a. establishing independence.
    b. understanding sexual feelings.
    c. developing relationships.
    d. all of these

3. Most people marry so that the new generation can be raised with their beliefs and values.

   a. true   b. false

4. The two qualities essential for a successful relationship are

   a. romantic love and attraction.
   b. passion and caring.
   c. financial security and respect.
   d. caring and respect.

5. Open communication between parent and teenager is the most important factor in their relationship.

   a. true   b. false

6. The developmental tasks facing adolescents are related to _____ and _____ issues.

   a. social, emotional
   b. moral, ethical
   c. a and b
   d. none of these

7. In order to progress successfully into adulthood, the adolescent must learn to

   a. be independent and separate from his or her parents.
   b. separate from his or her parents and bear children.
   c. bear children and be independent.
   d. none of these

8. Adolescence is probably less difficult now than it was in the past.

   a. true   b. false

9. Parents must learn to _____ their adolescents.

   a. allow complete freedom to
   b. set limits for
   c. condone the sexual freedom of
   d. not worry about

10. Fortunately, depression and suicide are not a major problem for adolescents.

    a. true   b. false

11. Adults have a responsibility to serve as role models for teenagers.

    a. true   b. false

12. People should look for individuals who have compatible beliefs, attitudes, and interests when choosing a mate.

    a. true   b. false

13. Remaining single is not widely accepted as an alternative to marriage.

    a. true   b. false

14. Recent studies indicate that there are more similarities in cohabitation and marriage than there are differences.

    a. true   b. false

15. Divorce rates have _____ since the 1950's.

    a. decreased slightly
    b. increased slightly
    c. almost doubled
    d. tripled

16. Although children definitely suffer when their parents divorce, most of them adjust well as time passes.

    a. true   b. false

17. Sound reasons for having children include children

    a. bringing more meaning and purpose to life.
    b. offering a unique opportunity to love and nurture.
    c. stabilizing an unhappy marriage.
    d. a and b

18. Healthy child development is fostered by a number of factors, including

    a. nurturance, love, and acceptance.
    b. competence and self-confidence.
    c. appropriate role models.
    d. a stimulating and responsive environment.
    e. all of these

19. To help the baby's successful emotional development, parents must first help the baby develop _____.

    a. intellect.
    b. physical health.
    c. basic trust.
    d. socialization.

20. Until children are about two years old, they are not active participants in the parent-child relationship.

a. true   b. false

21. Though much has been written about it, the traditional role of the mother really has not changed much in the last 50 years.

a. true   b. false

22. Financial pressures frequently place greater strains on the single parent than on the married couple.

a. true   b. false

23. Domestic violence, including child abuse, is limited to a very small segment of the population.

a. true   b. false

24. Solutions to the problem of child abuse are the responsibility of

a. parents.
b. physicians and teachers.
c. the courts.
d. everyone.

25. Some of the most significant problems encountered in intimate relationships are

a. differing ideas of intimacy.
b. division of labor.
c. money.
d. sex.
e. all of these

Answer Key

1. c (p. 169)
2. d (TV)
3. b (p. 172)
4. d (p. 172)
5. a (TV)
6. c (TV)
7. a (TV)
8. b (TV)
9. b (TV)
10. b (TV)
11. a (TV)
12. a (p. 174)
13. b (p. 174)

14. a (p. 177)
15. c (p. 177)
16. a (p. 178)
17. d (p. 179)
18. e (p. 179)
19. c (p. 180)
20. b (p. 181)
21. b (p. 182)
22. a (p. 184)
23. b (p. 186)
24. d (p. 187)
25. d (p. 190)

LESSON 9   "When Sex Was Good, It Was Very,
            Very Good; When It Was Bad..."

*"Condomophobia -- fear that a druggist will describe your purchase
over the store intercom. "*

**Johnny Carson
"The Tonight Show," February 13, 1987**

"Sexuality is the sum total of one's personality. "

Unknown

Learning Objectives

Knowledge

Upon successful completion of all assignments in this lesson, you should be able to

1. Distinguish between sex and sexuality and discuss the basis of sexuality and sexual behavior.

2. Discuss the origin of attitudes toward sex and explain how those attitudes may change over time.

3. Identify and describe the erogenous zones and the major external structures of the male and female anatomy.

4. Describe the four general stages of human sexual response and explain any differences between male and female responses.

5. Explain the various forms of sexual expression and discuss why responsible sexual expression is important.

6. Identify and explain various male and female dysfunctions and discuss methods for dealing with sexual dysfunctions.

7. Discuss information necessary to the therapist counseling individuals with sexual dysfunctions.

8. List and discuss some of the ethical standards that apply to professionals treating sexual problems.

Attitude

1. Analyze your own opinions on sexuality and describe ways (if any) in which they were changed by this lesson.

2. Describe your own feelings about what responsibilities are part of a full expression of sexuality.

Overview

Of all aspects of health, sexuality is most surrounded by myths and misunderstandings. It has been only in recent times that we have talked openly about sexual matters and concerns. Even now sexual topics are the objects of innuendos, jokes, and exaggerations. It is hoped that future generations will be able to communicate honestly and openly about this important part of everybody's well-being.

Contrary to commonly held myths, the sexual response of males is really not so different from that of females. Also, we now realize how very important emotions, relationships, and communication are to a healthy sexual relationship. It's been said that "the most important sex organ is between the ears"; in other words, the mind is as important to the sexual response as the genitals are.

Although our beliefs have changed about which variant sexual behavior is acceptable, the concept that "anything goes" is not widely accepted or thought of as healthy. Our decisions about sexual behavior need to help us nurture and develop relationships, rather than hurt or degrade them. If you make these positive decisions, communicate openly, and truly value the relationship, your sexuality will reflect the very best of human intimacy.

Study Assignments

Textbook - Chapter 8, "Human Sexuality," pp. 197-223

TV - Program 9, "When Sex Was Good, It Was Very, Very Good; When It Was Bad..."

Complete Self-Assessment, "What Are Your Attitudes About Sex?" on pp. 212-213 in the text.

Key Terms

sex (p. 197)
sexuality (p. 197)
erogenous zones (p. 202)
penis (p. 203)
urethra (p. 203)
glans (p. 203)
coronal ridge (p. 203)
frenulum (p. 203)
scrotum (p. 203)

perineum (p. 204)

vulva (p. 204)

mons veneris (p. 204)

labia (p. 204)

clitoris (p. 204)

vagina (p. 204)

hymen (p. 204)

vasocongestion (p. 206)

myotonia (p. 206)

spermatic cords (p. 206)

orgasm (p. 207)

ejaculation (p. 207)

refractory period (p. 208)

circumcision (p. 208)

foreskin (p. 208)

masturbation (p. 210)

foreplay (p. 211)

homosexuality (p. 213)

heterosexuality (p. 213)

sexual dysfunction (p. 216, TV)

premature ejaculation (p. 216)

retarded ejaculation (p. 216)

impotence (p. 217)

primary impotence (p. 217)

secondary impotence (p. 217)

anorgasmia (p. 219)

primary anorgasmia (p. 219)

secondary anorgasmia (p. 219)

situational anorgasmia (p. 219)

dyspareunia (p. 219)

vaginismus (p. 219)

Text Focus Questions

1. Explain sexuality. Why do men act in certain ways? Women?

2. How do people learn their attitudes toward sex and sexuality?

3. What are erogenous zones? Why do certain areas of the anatomy become associated with sexual response while others do not?

4. Describe the male and the female sexual anatomy.

5. List and explain the stages of sexual response.

6. What are some of the most common myths and misconceptions about sexual response?

7. Discuss the various acceptable forms of sexual expression.

8. What forms of sexual behavior are unacceptable? Why?

9. Explain the most common sexual dysfunctions and their treatment.

10. What does the term responsible sex mean? Why is important for people to approach sex responsibly?

TV Focus Questions

1. What are some of the problems that exist or that can develop in a sexual relationship?

2. How are some of the common sexual dysfunctions related to age? What are the most common symptoms?

3. What are the most useful pieces of information a therapist must obtain in order to help individuals with sexual dysfunctions?

4. What are the ethical standards of therapists treating sexual problems?

5. What specific methods are used to treat sexual dysfunctions?

Optional Strengthening Exercises

1. Interview a sexual therapist to learn more about sexual problems and their treatment.

2. Develop a list of community agencies that treat sexual problems.

3. Find out how a rape crisis center operates and the legal aspects of a rape investigation.

Self Test

1. The basis of sexuality is both biological and learned.

   a. true   b. false

2. The fundamental sense of oneself as a male or a female is known as

   a. self-concept.
   b. androgyny.
   c. heterosexuality.
   d. core gender identity.

3. The social conditioning that shaped the "typical" man and woman of the past has not changed.

    a. true   b. false

4. People have what might be called a psychosexual response that integrates their

    a. psychological and intellectual reactions.
    b. attitudes and needs.
    c. physical and psychological reactions.
    d. attitudes and learned responses.

5. It is a mistake to think that everyone has the same patterns of sexual arousal and that gratifying sex results from merely learning the proper erogenous zones to stimulate.

    a. true   b. false

6. Several parts of both the male and the female sexual anatomy function reproductively as well as to produce pleasure during sexual arousal.

    a. true   b. false

7. The _____ is a canal-like structure that is a responsive muscular organ.

    a. scrotum
    b. glans
    c. ovary
    d. vagina

8. Masters and Johnson discovered more similarities than differences in the sexual responses of men and women.

   a. true   b. false

9. The stage of sexual response characterized by lubrication of the vagina and the clitoris, resulting in enlargement of the vagina in the female and causing an erection of the penis in the male, is

   a. excitement.
   b. plateau.
   c. orgasmic.
   d. resolution.

10. A woman can usually achieve multiple orgasms in a relatively short period of time, while the man usually experiences only one.

    a. true   b. false

11. The phase just preceding orgasm when all sensations become intensified is

    a. excitement.
    b. plateau.
    c. orgasmic.
    d. resolution.

12. The gradual return of sexual organs, blood pressure, heart rate, and breathing to normality marks the _____ phase.

    a. excitement.
    b. plateau.
    c. orgasmic.
    d. resolution.

13. Circumcision usually influences sexual pleasure and behavior.

    a. true   b. false

14. Masturbation is one of the most misunderstood forms of sexuality and is a very normal part of the developing sexual expression of the individual.

    a. true   b. false

15. Petting and foreplay are really not very important in the communication of our sexual feelings.

    a. true   b. false

16. Emotional or erotic attraction to, and behavior with, a member of the same sex is

    a. transsexuality.
    b. homosexuality.
    c. transvestism.
    d. bisexuality.

17. Though rape is sometimes seen as a type of sexual activity, it is as much an act of violence and anger.

    a. true   b. false

18. The cause(s) of sexual dysfunction is/are

    a. physical problem(s).
    b. psychological problem(s).
    c. communication.
    d. all of these

19. Sexual dysfunctions occur in about _____ of all couples.

    a. 5%
    b. 20%
    c. 50%
    d. 100%

20. Ejaculatory problems in the male are frequently age related, premature ejaculation occurring in younger men and delayed ejaculation in older men.

    a. true   b. false

21. Female sexual response develops during adolescence and then decreases rather dramatically after age 30.

    a. true   b. false

22. The most common cause of decreased desire for intercourse is

    a. emotional.
    b. physical.
    c. anxiety related.
    d. none of these

23. In treating patients with sexual problems, it is important for the therapist to

    a. get a clear picture of what is happening.
    b. take a careful history.
    c. obtain a thorough physical exam report from the clients.
    d. all of these

24. Incest and child abuse are increasingly being recognized as major problems in our society.

    a. true   b. false

25. Today, with the prevalence of AIDS and other sexually transmitted diseases, a greater responsibility between partners is necessary.

    a. true   b. false

Answer Key

1. a (p. 197)	14. a (p. 210)
2. d (p. 198)	15. b (p. 211)
3. b (p. 199)	16. b (p. 213)
4. c (p. 199)	17. a (pp. 214-215)
5. a (p. 202)	18. d (p. 216, TV)
6. a (pp. 203-204)	19. c (TV)
7. d (p. 204)	20. a (pp. 216-217)
8. a (p. 206)	21. b (TV)
9. a (p. 206)	22. a (TV)
10. a (p. 208)	23. d (TV)
11. b (p. 206)	24. a (p. 215)
12. d (p. 208)	25. a (p. 221)
13. b (p. 208)	

LESSON 10　　From Puberty To Menopause

Each sex seemed to have half the loaf and was very uncomfortable about the half they were missing. Did the missing halves even belong to the same loaf? Men had the credentials with which to barter for external advancement. Women had the perceptiveness to say "what good is becoming president if you lose touch with your family and your feelings?"

The woman was jealous of the man's credentials. The man was disturbed by the woman's truth.

Gail Sheehy, *Passages*

Learning Objectives

Knowledge

Upon successful completion of all assignments in this lesson, you should be able to

1. List the major parts of the male and the female reproductive systems and describe their functions.

2. Identify the various contraceptive methods, explaining the benefits and drawbacks of each, including the techniques used in natural family planning.

3. Discuss the importance of planning for pregnancy and describe the beginnings of pregnancy and the development of a fetus.

4. Identify and explain various techniques for terminating a pregnancy and discuss attitudes toward abortion.

5. Discuss the choices parents must make in preparing for childbirth and describe the stages of labor.

6. Describe the most common problems of the female reproductive system.

7. Explain the changes in the female at the time of menopause.

Attitude

1. Discuss the reasons for your beliefs concerning artificial processes of fertilization.

2. Understand and accept the complexities of both sides of the abortion issue.

Overview

If you have or plan to have a sexual relationship, this lesson is particularly important. A sexual relationship without understanding contraception and the reproductive systems of both men and women is like taking a very hot sports car for a spin without learning to drive. Lack of knowledge and irresponsibility result in sexually transmitted diseases, problem pregnancy, unwanted children, and child abuse. Knowledge, understanding, and responsible behavior result in mature relationships.

There is nothing more remarkable than the growth of a single cell into a perfectly formed human infant. When one considers how many things can happen in the process of conception, the development of the embryo into a fetus, and the growth of the fetus during pregnancy, the remarkable becomes a true miracle. Many people are disheartened to see this miraculous process devalued by the attitudes a number of others seem to have about sexual matters.

If you take nothing else from this lesson, you need to review or to learn for the first time how reproductive systems work, especially when a woman is most likely to conceive and how to prevent unwanted pregnancy. (Hope is not a method of birth control.) Most unwanted pregnancies, it seems, occur when couples use no form of birth control. There are no easy solutions to the problem of an unwanted pregnancy. Simply put, if you don't want pregnancy to occur, use some means of birth control. Such birth control is the responsibility of both partners! Utilize the information from this lesson to begin developing personal values about your own sexual behavior or to change old ideas you may have developed earlier in an uninformed situation.

Study Assignments

Textbook - Chapter 9, "Reproduction And Sexual Health," pp. 225-254

TV - Program 10, "From Puberty To Menopause"

Key Terms

ovum (ova) (p. 226)
ovaries (p. 226)
menarche (p. 226)
ovulation (p. 226)
Fallopian tubes (oviducts) (p. 227)
uterus (p. 227)
cervix (p. 227)
endometrium (p. 227)
menstrual cycle (p. 227)
menstruation (p. 227)
prostaglandin (p. 228)
premenstrual syndrome (PMS) (p. 228, TV)
menopause (p. 229, TV)
climacteric (p. 229)

testes (testicles) (p. 230)
sperm (p. 230)
spermatogenesis (p. 230)
epididymis (p. 230)
vas deferens (p. 231)
seminal vesicles (p. 231)
prostate gland (p. 231)
semen (p. 231)
seminal fluid (p. 231)
ejaculatory ducts (p. 231)
Cowper's glands (p. 231)
condom (p. 233)
oral contraceptives (p. 234)
intrauterine device (IUD) (p. 235)
diaphragm (p. 236)
vasectomy (p. 238)
tubal ligation (p. 238)
contraceptive implant (p. 239)
vaginal rings (p. 239)
injectable contraceptives (p. 239)
vaginal condom (p. 239)
amniocentesis (p. 242)
chorionic villi sampling (p. 242)
placenta (p. 243)
prenatal (p. 243)
umbilical cord (p. 243)
amnion (amniotic sac) (p. 243)
Rh factor (p. 244)
fetal alcohol syndrome (FAS) (p. 245)
toxemia (p. 246)
preeclampsia (p. 246)
eclampsia (p. 246)
spontaneous abortion (p. 246)
abortion (p. 247)

episiotomy (p. 250)
caesarean section (p. 250)

Text Focus Questions

1. Name and describe the functions of the female reproductive organs.

2. Explain the menstrual cycle.

3. What physical changes come about in menopause?

4. Name and describe the functions of the male reproductive organs.

5. Trace the sperm's path from its formation to its uniting with the female ovum/egg in conception. Do the same with the ovum from its formation to its uniting with the sperm.

6. Describe in detail and compare the various methods of birth control in terms of effectiveness, duration, acceptability, and safety.

7. What are some of the trends in contraceptives for the future?

8. What are some of the considerations facing the couple planning for pregnancy?

9. Explain the development of the fetus from fertilization to birth.

10. How should a woman care for her health during pregnancy?

11. Describe some common problems of pregnancy.

12. What are the methods used for terminating a pregnancy and at what stages of pregnancy can each be used?

13. Describe the birth process.

TV Focus Questions

1. What causes menstrual "cramps"?

2. What is premenstrual syndrome (PMS) and what are typical symptoms of this condition?

3. What are some of the most common problems of the female reproductive system?

4. Define menopause.

5. What are the symptoms and treatment of osteoporosis?

Optional Strengthening Exercises

1. Research the topic of in vitro fertilization and make some decisions concerning your own beliefs about this controversial topic.

2. Interview proponents of both sides of the abortion issue and recognize your own values about the issue.

Self Test

1. The ovaries produce

   a. semen.
   b. eggs.
   c. menstrual fluid.
   d. none of these

2. The Fallopian tubes are attached to the ovaries as well as to the uterus.

   a. true   b. false

3. _____ is manufactured within the ovaries as part of the menstrual cycle.

   a. A follicle-stimulating hormone
   b. A luteinizing hormone
   c. Estrogen
   d. Seminal fluid

4. The psychological effects of the menstrual cycle are at least in part due to dramatic changes in the levels of hormones that act on the whole body.

   a. true   b. false

5. During menopause a woman's sexual life ends.

   a. true   b. false

6. Sperm are produced in the

   a. glans penis.
   b. Bartholin's glands.
   c. Bulbourethral (Cowper's) glands.
   d. testes.

7. The vas deferens is a cordlike structure that forms sperm.

   a. true   b. false

8. The final passage for both urine and semen in the male is the urethra, which begins at the bottom of the urinary bladder and ends in a small opening at the end of the penis.

   a. true   b. false

9. Condoms, diaphragms, and sponges are barrier contraceptives that are quite effective, but some couples consider them inconvenient.

   a. true   b. false

10. The oral contraceptive is one of the most effective means of contraception, but it has some risk.

    a. true   b. false

11. Sterilizations by vasectomy or tubal ligation are easily reversed by a simple surgical procedure.

    a. true   b. false

12. By the third week after a missed period, signs of pregnancy are apparent during a pelvic exam.

    a. true   b. false

13. By the end of the third month of pregnancy, the fetus

    a. is about three inches long.
    b. kicks its legs, closes its fingers, and turns its head.
    c. has internal organs that function.
    d. all of these

14. A woman who smokes, drinks, or is addicted to drugs has a much higher risk of having a baby with problems.

    a. true   b. false

15. Some conditions common to pregnancy that can usually be treated quite easily are all of these *except*

    a. morning sickness.
    b. heartburn.
    c. eclampsia.
    d. constipation.

16. The surgical procedure of removing the baby through an incision in the lower part of the abdominal wall and uterus is a/an

    a. episiotomy.
    b. caesarean section.
    c. laporotomy.
    d. vasectomy.

17. The bursting of the amniotic sac and the appearance of fluid usually indicate that labor is complete.

    a. true   b. false

18. The birth of the baby signals the end of the birth process.

    a. true   b. false

19. In order to decrease the symptoms of PMS, the woman is encouraged to

    a.   reduce salt intake.
    b.   avoid a high sugar intake and eat small meals.
    c.   avoid stress and get adequate rest.
    d.   all of these

20. Osteoporosis is a condition found in about 50 percent of women and is characterized by deterioration of bone tissue.

    a.   true   b.   false

Answer Key

1.	b (p. 226)	11.	b (p. 238, TV)
2.	b (p. 226)	12.	a (p. 244)
3.	c (p. 227)	13.	d (p. 243)
4.	a (p. 228)	14.	a (p. 245)
5.	b (p. 229)	15.	c (p. 246)
6.	d (p. 230)	16.	b (p. 250)
7.	b (pp. 230-231)	17.	b (p. 250)
8.	a (p. 231)	18.	b (p. 252)
9.	a (pp. 233-235, TV)	19.	d (TV)
10.	a (p. 234, TV)	20.	a (TV)

LESSON 11   AIDS

"AIDS could become the plague of this century."

Wyatt Rousseau, M.D., in 1983

Learning Objectives

Knowledge

Upon successful completion of all assignments in this lesson, you should be able to

1. Explain the effects lifestyle, travel, and medical progress can have on patterns of diseases.

2. Describe what an infection is and explain the role of agents, hosts, and environmental factors in a communicable disease.

3. Identify and describe the primary agents of a communicable disease.

4. Describe how the body defends itself against infection, including first-line defenses, the inflammatory response, and immunity.

5. Identify major sexually transmitted diseases and describe their symptoms and potential effects.

6. List the symptoms of human immunodeficiency virus (HIV) infection, AIDS-related complex, and AIDS; identify the primary modes of transmission of the HIV virus and the primary preventive measures for AIDS.

7. Discuss the emotional implications of AIDS.

Attitude

1. Examine your own sexual behavior in relation to the risks involving the various sexually transmitted diseases. Make conscious decisions concerning the level of risk you are willing to take.

Overview

The great epidemics of the past are for the most part being controlled by antibiotics or eliminated by vaccines. Thanks to modern medical technology, the organisms that caused these diseases have been isolated, classified, and contained. Though some serious communicable diseases still pose a threat to less developed countries, they are for the most part little threat to large segments of the population of the United States.

The frightening exceptions to this decline are the sexually transmitted diseases that are epidemic in our populations, affecting more people than any other disease except the common cold. Even though most sexually transmitted diseases (STDs) are curable, the numbers of people infected increases every day. Due to changing social mores and values, these diseases are out of control.

Though most STDs are curable, medical science cannot control this epidemic as it has epidemics in the past. Each individual must examine his/her own sexual behavior and take necessary precautions to help stop the spread of the diseases. Anyone can contract any of the STDs (including AIDS, which is becoming the deadliest disease of the century) by sexual contact with an infected person. AIDS, once thought to be a disease confined to homosexuals and intravenous drug users, is now seen in the heterosexual, non-drug-using population. Such measures as limiting one's sexual partners and using condoms regularly will help control this epidemic.

The control of communicable disease is a perfect example of the advances being made in scientific medicine. However, much of the responsibility for control lies with the individual. Medicine can't do everything.

Study Assignments

Textbook - Chapter 10, "Communicable Diseases," pp. 257-285

TV - Program 11, "AIDS"

Complete Self-Assessment, "What Is Your Attitude Toward Sickness?" on p. 261 in the text.

Key Terms

iatrogenic (p. 259)
nosocomial (p. 259)
agent factor (p. 261)
host factor (p. 261)
environmental factor (p. 262)
incubation period (p. 262)
prodrome period (p. 262)
clinical disease (p. 262)
decline stage (p. 262)
convalescence (p. 262)
carrier (p. 262)
endogenous (p. 262)
exogenous (p. 262)
pathogen (p. 262)
bacterium (bacteria) (p. 263)
virus (p. 265)
interferon (p. 265)

rickettsiae (p. 267)
vector (p. 267)
fungi (p. 267)
prion (p. 268)
inflammation (p. 269)
inflammatory response (p. 269)
phagocytes (p. 269)
abscess (p. 270)
immunity (p. 270)
lymphocytes (p. 270)
antibodies (p. 270)
antigens (p. 271)
vaccine (p. 272)
active immunity (p. 272)
passive immunity (p. 272)
gamma globulin (p. 272)
toxoids (p. 273)
sexually transmitted diseases (STDs) (p. 275, TV)
pelvic inflammatory disease (PID) (p. 275)
acquired immune deficiency syndrome (AIDS) (p. 279, TV)

Text Focus Questions

1. How has the changing lifestyle of people affected the incidence of disease?

2. Explain the relationships of agent, host, and environment in the cause of illness.

3. Describe the course of an infectious disease.

4. List and describe the major types of organisms that cause disease.

5. How does the body defend itself against infectious disease?

6. Why is the immune system especially important? What are some of the conditions particularly related to the immune system failing to function effectively?

7. List and describe the risks, symptoms, and treatments of the major sexually transmitted diseases.

8. Why is acquired immune deficiency syndrome (AIDS) such a threat in the world today? How is AIDS different from syphilis, gonorrhea, and some of the STDs that were a major problem in the past years?

9. How can AIDS be prevented? List some of the common-sense preventive measures that can be taken by everyone.

10. How are politics affecting the treatment and future of AIDS?

TV Focus Questions

1. What kinds of emotional issues must patients and families dealing with AIDS face?

2. What social, moral, and ethical concerns are impacted by AIDS?

3. How accurate is testing for AIDS?

Optional Strengthening Exercises

1. Talk with someone who had tuberculosis many years ago about the treatment used before modern antibiotics. Compare that with the treatment used now.

2. Interview someone who works in an AIDS clinic or counseling center and find out what problems AIDS patients face.

Self Test

1. Diseases that can be transmitted from person to person, directly or indirectly, are called _____ and are caused by organisms known as _____.

   a. chronic, bacteria
   b. communicable, viruses
   c. communicable, pathogens
   d. chronic, pathogens

2. Though lifestyle has changed much through the years, the nature of disease has not changed significantly.

   a. true   b. false

3. _____ include the organisms that cause an infectious disease.

   a. Environmental factors
   b. Host factors
   c. Agent factors

4. In order, the stages of a disease are

   a. prodrome, incubation, decline, convalescence, clinical.
   b. clinical, incubation, prodrome, convalescence, decline.
   c. incubation, prodrome, clinical, decline, convalescence.
   d. clinical, prodrome, incubation, convalescence, decline.

5. _____ is/are not one of the five basic types of pathogens.

   a. Bacteria
   b. Molecules
   c. Virus
   d. Rickettsiae
   e. Fungi
   f. Prions

6. The pathogen that secretes a disease-causing toxin producing such diseases as syphilis, tuberculosis, and rheumatic fever is a

   a. fungus.
   b. protozoan.
   c. parasitic worm.
   d. bacterium.
   e. virus.

7. One of the smallest of the pathogens, a _____ causes colds, flu, rabies, and polio.

   a. virus
   b. bacterium
   c. rickettsia
   d. protozoan
   e. fungus

8. Athlete's foot and vaginal yeast infections are caused by the pathogen known as a

   a. protozoan.
   b. virus.
   c. rickettsia.
   d. prion.
   e. fungus.

9. Infectious mononucleosis is caused by _____, and symptoms often mimic serious diseases.

   a. bacteria
   b. rickettsiae
   c. protozoans
   d. viruses

10. _____ is/are the body's first effective line(s) of defense against disease.

   a. Inflammation
   b. Immunity
   c. Interferon
   d. The skin and mucous membranes

11. _____ provide(s) an important defense against foreign matter and microorganisms.

   a. The inflammatory response
   b. The immune system
   c. Epithelial defenses
   d. Interferon

12. _____, the body's third line of defense, helps protect against specific diseases.

   a. Interferon
   b. Immunity
   c. The epithelium
   d. Inflammatory process

13. In the immune mechanism, as in the inflammatory response, white blood cells known as _____ become involved in fighting infection.

   a. antibodies
   b. hemoglobin
   c. lymphocytes
   d. none of these

14. An inherent lack of susceptibility to a disease is called

   a. acquired immunity.
   b. resistance.
   c. natural immunity.
   d. none of these

15. Because so many of the communicable diseases have been eradicated, it is no longer important to have children immunized against disease.

   a. true   b. false

16. In spite of the decline in most communicable diseases, the rate of _____ is increasing.

   a. polio
   b. chicken pox
   c. sexually transmitted diseases
   d. toxic shock syndrome

17. There are two forms of herpes, one causing "cold sores" and the other causing genital herpes.

   a. true   b. false

18. The highest incidence of STDs is in

   a. those under 25.
   b. minorities.
   c. the medically underserved.
   d. all of these

19. Until AIDS, _____ was the most serious and deadly STD.

   a. gonorrhea
   b. chlamydia
   c. syphilis
   d. toxic shock syndrome

20. If left untreated, syphilis will disappear.

   a. true   b. false

21. One of the greatest dangers of gonorrhea is the chance that it can affect the baby's eyes at childbirth.

   a. true   b. false

22. The victim of _____ has a suppressed immune system, unattributable to any other known cause.

    a. syphilis
    b. AIDS
    c. toxic shock syndrome
    d. gonorrhea

23. In the later stages of AIDS, the patient will frequently succumb to opportunistic diseases not normally seen in people whose immune systems are functioning.

    a. true   b. false

24. The diagnostic tests for the HIV virus are very accurate, particularly at six months after being exposed.

    a. true   b. false

25. Individuals who want to lessen their risk of contracting an STD should

    a. limit their number of sexual partners.
    b. use a condom during intercourse.
    c. avoid any contact with an infected person or one suspected to be infected.
    d. seek medical attention if there is question of infection.
    e. all of these

26. AIDS occurs only among adult homosexuals.

    a. true   b. false

27. AIDS has drawn attention to the need for more hospice care.

 a. true b. false

28. The financial and emotional burden of AIDS is much less severe than the physical one.

 a. true b. false

29. There are many controversial political issues involving AIDS.

 a. true b. false

Answer Key

1. c (pp. 257, 262)
2. b (p. 258)
3. c (p. 261)
4. c (p. 262)
5. b (pp. 263-268)
6. d (pp. 263-264)
7. a (pp. 265-267)
8. e (p. 267)
9. d (p. 267)
10. d (p. 268)
11. a (p. 269)
12. b (p. 270)
13. c (p. 270)
14. c (p. 271)
15. b (p. 274)
16. c (p. 275)
17. a (p. 276)
18. d (p. 275)
19. c (p. 277)
20. b (p. 277)
21. a (p. 278)
22. b (p. 279)
23. a (p. 280)
24. a (TV)
25. e (pp. 280-281)
26. b (TV)
27. a (TV)
28. b (TV)
29. a (p. 283)

LESSON 12   Hypertension: Your Blood Pressure Is Showing

"It's supposed to be a professional secret, but I'll tell you anyway. We doctors do nothing. We only help and encourage the doctor within."

Albert Schweitzer
reprinted in *An Invitation to Health*, 3rd ed.

Learning Objectives

Knowledge

Upon successful completion of all assignments in this lesson, you should be able to

1. Identify the components and structures of the heart and circulatory system and explain how they work.

2. Explain hypertension and discuss its cause and treatment.

3. Define atherosclerosis and discuss its cause and treatment.

4. Explain systolic and diastolic blood pressure, including the normal limits for these.

Attitude

1. Describe lifestyle habits you practice that are related to the risk of hypertension, noting whether each is a positive or negative force.

Overview

Lessons 12, 13, and 14 all are related to cardiovascular health and conditions of the heart and blood vessels. In order to fully comprehend these lessons, it is important to understand the anatomy and physiology of the heart and vascular system. Remember, the heart is a pump sending the blood to the various organs, and the vessels form the pipelines that carry the blood. Arteries carry blood (usually oxygenated) away from the heart, and veins carry deoxygenated blood back to the heart. The only real exception to this is pulmonary circulation; the pulmonary arteries carry deoxygenated blood to the lungs, where it is oxygenated before being returned to the heart via the pulmonary veins.

At the time when antibiotics and vaccines were beginning to control most communicable disease, the number of fatalities from cardiovascular disease was rising dramatically. Today, people are more aware of the risk factor and practice better health habits, thereby reversing the trend. Nowhere are good health habits more important than in maintaining good cardiovascular health.

The good health habits that you have been studying in previous lessons apply to cardiovascular health as well. The importance of diet, exercise, smoking cessation, and alcohol moderation cannot be stressed enough! As with other aspects of health, there are risk factors that cannot be controlled. However, some of the most important ones are within the control of each individual. Though these health habits should begin in childhood, it is never too late to start.

High blood pressure (hypertension) has received much attention in recent years because 1) it affects large segments of the population, 2) generally it gives no outward symptoms, and 3) most cases of hypertension can be controlled with good health habits and medication. It is extremely important to monitor your blood pressure and make certain that it remains in the low-risk range.

These three lessons will focus on diseases with complicated names and sometimes confusing symptoms. The key knowledge for you to gain and implement, however, is how to practice health habits designed to minimize your risk of disease.

Study Assignments

Textbook - Chapter 11, "Cardiovascular Health And Disease," pp. 287-296

TV - Program 12, "Hypertension: Your Blood Pressure Is Showing"

Complete Self-Assessment, "Examine Your RISKO Score for Heart Disease Risks," on pp. 292-293 in the text.

Key Terms

aorta (p. 289)
pacemaker (p. 289)
arteries (p. 289)
capillaries (p. 289)
veins (p. 289)
blood pressure (p. 290)
hypertension (p. 290)
atherosclerosis (p.294)
plaque (p. 295)
thrombus (p. 295)
ischemia (p. 296)
thrombosis (p. 296)
embolus (p. 296)
embolism (p. 296)

Text Focus Questions

1. What is the function of the heart and how do its parts work to accomplish this function?

2. What are the functions of the circulatory system?

3. What is hypertension and why is it called the silent killer?

4. What are some of the causes of hypertension?

5. How is hypertension treated?

6. What is atherosclerosis and what causes this disease?

7. Explain the role of fats and cholesterol in atherosclerosis and other cardiovascular diseases.

TV Focus Questions

1. What is the function of blood pressure?

2. What are some of the complications of hypertension and physiologically how do these occur?

3. Name factors that cause blood pressure to vary among healthy individuals.

4. What are some of the causes of high blood pressure?

5. How is stress related to hypertension?

6. Why is it sometimes difficult to treat hypertension effectively?

7. Name the lifestyle habits important in lowering the risk of hypertension.

Optional Strengthening Exercise

1. Have your blood pressure checked several times during the next few weeks and compare the readings with normal ranges. Take appropriate actions on your findings. Appropriate actions are described in your textbook and in the video. If you have any doubts, ask your physician, college health center personnel, or your instructor.

Self Test

1. _____ is/are manifestation(s) of cardiovascular disease.

   a. Heart attacks
   b. Coronary artery disease
   c. Stroke and high blood pressure
   d. a and b only
   e. a, b, and c only

2. Cardiovascular diseases are chronic, degenerative disorders that take years or even decades to develop.

   a. true   b. false

3. There is no good evidence that lifestyle is related to cardiovascular disease.

   a. true   b. false

4. Some of the primary risk factors related to cardiovascular disease are

    a. cigarette smoking and high intake of cholesterol.
    b. too little exercise and hypertension.
    c. obesity.
    d. all of these

5. Deaths from cardiovascular disease are now

    a. increasing.
    b. declining.
    c. stabilizing.

6. The heart is actually "heart" shaped and is found to the right of the body's midline.

    a. true   b. false

7. Most of the heart is muscle tissue, enabling it to act as a pump to circulate blood.

    a. true   b. false

8. There are _____ chambers in the heart.

    a. 2
    b. 3
    c. 4
    d. 6

9. As the heart beats, the _____ atrium and _____ ventricle work together to form one pump while the _____ atrium and _____ ventricle form the other.

   a. left, right, left, right
   b. right, left, right, left
   c. left, left, right, right
   d. right, left, left, right

10. The _____ in the heart regulates the heartbeat by stimulating the heart muscles to pump in a coordinated fashion.

    a. endocardium
    b. electrocardium
    c. pericardium
    d. pacemaker

11. The circulatory system consists of the heart and blood vessels leading to and from it.

    a. true   b. false

12. Generally speaking, arteries carry oxygenated blood away from the heart, and veins carry deoxygenated blood.

    a. true   b. false

13. Hypertension is a persistent _____ in blood pressure that _____ the risk of cardiovascular disease.

    a. elevation, lowers
    b. decrease, lowers
    c. elevation, increases
    d. decrease, increases

14. Hypertension is called the silent killer because it frequently presents no obvious symptoms.

    a. true   b. false

15. Atherosclerosis is a condition that results in impaired flow of blood through the vessels.

    a. true   b. false

16. Damaged walls of the blood vessels in _____ cause them to attract fatty debris and cause a buildup of plaque.

    a. atherosclerosis
    b. arteriosclerosis
    c. embolism
    d. none of these

17. LDL (low-density lipoprotein), one of the substances in the blood, seems to inhibit the accumulation of cholesterol in the arteries.

    a. true   b. false

18. _____ carry excess cholesterol away from the cells and back to the liver, where it is metabolized and excreted.

    a. Low-density lipoproteins (LDLs)
    b. Thrombi
    c. High-density lipoproteins (HDLs)
    d. Plasma molecules

19. Generally the heart can continue pumping effectively even through arteries that have been reduced as much as _____ percent in size.

    a. 20
    b. 90
    c. 40
    d. 60

20. When a blood clot or piece of plaque breaks off from an arterial wall and becomes wedged in a narrowed vessel elsewhere in the body, the resulting condition is

    a. thrombis.
    b. plaque.
    c. gangrene.
    d. embolism.

21. The causative factors in high blood pressure include

    a. high salt intake.
    b. genetics.
    c. disease processes.
    d. obesity.
    e. all of these

22. A health habit important to reducing the risks of hypertension is

    a. lowering salt intake.
    b. maintaining an ideal weight.
    c. exercising daily.
    d. consuming alcohol moderately.
    e. learning to relax.
    f. all of these

Answer Key

1. e (p. 287)
2. a (p. 287)
3. b (p. 287)
4. d (p. 287)
5. b (p. 287)
6. b (p. 289)
7. a (p. 289)
8. c (p. 289)
9. c (p. 289)
10. d (p. 289)
11. a (p. 289)
12. a (p. 289)
13. c (p. 291, TV)
14. a (p. 291, TV)
15. a (p. 295)
16. a (p. 295)
17. b (p. 295)
18. c (p. 295)
19. d (p. 296)
20. d (p. 296)
21. e (TV)
22. f (TV)

LESSON 13 Heart Attack

"Each of us stands alone at the heart of the Earth
Pierced through by a ray of sunlight:
And suddenly it's evening."

Salvatore Quasimodo
reprinted in *Human Development*, 2nd ed.

Learning Objectives

Knowledge

Upon successful completion of all assignments in this lesson, you should be able to

1. Explain the possible causes, symptoms, and treatment of heart attack (myocardial infarction).

2. Describe the role of cardiopulmonary resuscitation (CPR) in the treatment of heart attack.

3. Discuss stroke (cerebrovascular accident), including how it occurs, underlying causes, and potential consequences.

4. Describe cardiovascular diseases other than heart attack and stroke.

5. Discuss the psychological effects of heart attack.

6. Identify some of the newest treatments for heart attack.

133

7. Explain the relationship of personal responsibility for health and risk for heart attack.

8. Describe some successful community education projects designed to lower the risk of cardiovascular disease.

Attitude

1. Assess your own risks of developing heart disease based on your lifestyle and family history.

Overview

Through most of this course healthy lifestyles, designed to prevent chronic illness, have been considered. This lesson discusses the most common serious cardiovascular conditions that those healthy lifestyles are designed to minimize.

Heart attacks and strokes are among the most frightening medical conditions that can occur. Though cardiovascular diseases kill more Americans than does any other illness, it is important to remember that many people survive these conditions and recover to lead normal lives. Some vital components in the survival of these patients are the number of people trained in CPR, high-quality emergency medical services (EMS), modern medical technology, new techniques in surgery, and excellent rehabilitation programs. Of course the role of lifestyle modification to minimize the risks of these conditions cannot be stressed enough.

Modern medical treatment and surgery have helped save the lives of many victims of cardiovascular disease. Treatments not even thought of 25 years ago are routinely used today. One of the most important techniques used is a relatively simple one that is easily learned by any lay-person. This technique, cardiopulmonary resuscitation, is a method of breathing for a patient and compressing the heart rhythmically to cause the blood to circulate and to get the heart beating again. One important part of healthy living is to learn CPR. For example, if you know the symptoms of a heart attack and are trained in CPR, you may be able to save a life. Make knowledge of CPR a part of your healthy lifestyle plan.

As we discuss illness and pathology in this lesson, some students may think the course is a "watered-down medical school." Definitely not; the illnesses discussed are important for every individual to be familiar with.

Study Assignments

Textbook - Chapter 11, "Cardiovascular Health And Disease," pp. 296-305

TV - Program 13, "Heart Attack"

Key Terms

heart attack (p. 296, TV)
myocardial infarction (p. 296)
myocardial ischemia (p. 296)
angina pectoris (p. 296)
coronary thrombosis (p. 297)
coronary embolism (p. 297)
cardiac arrest (p. 297)
cardiopulmonary resuscitation (CPR) (p. 298, study guide)
collateral circulation (p. 300)
stroke (p. 300)
cerebral thrombosis (p. 300)
cerebral embolism (p. 300)
cerebral hemorrhage (p. 300)
transient ischemic attack (TIA) (p. 300)

angioplasty (p. 303, TV)
bypass surgery (p. 303)
arrhythmia (p. 303)
ventricular fibrillation (p. 304)
rheumatic fever (p. 304)
congestive heart failure (p. 305)
edema (p. 305)
TPA (TV)
cardiac catherization (TV)

Text Focus Questions

1. What is angina pectoris? What is its significance?

2. How does a heart attack happen? What are its symptoms?

3. How is cardiopulmonary resuscitation important to the treatment of heart attack?

4. What are the important aspects of recovery from a heart attack? Why?

5. What happens during a stroke or cerebrovascular accident? What are some common underlying causes for most strokes?

6. Why is it important to stress early diagnosis of potential cardiovascular problems? List some of the exams used.

7. List and describe some of the major cardiovascular diseases other than heart attack and stroke.

TV Focus Questions

1. What are some of the psychological aspects of heart attack?

2. How does TPA work in the treatment of heart attack?

3. What are some other treatments for heart attack?

4. What are some of the lifestyle modifications crucial in recovering from a heart attack or preventing a heart attack?

5. How are some communities working to lower the cardiovascular disease risk for their citizens?

Optional Strengthening Exercise

1. Contact your college health center, American Heart Association, or American Red Cross and enroll in a CPR course.

Self Test

1. Obstruction of one or more coronary arteries is the leading cause of myocardial ischemia.

   a. true   b. false

2. The severe gripping chest pain caused by the heart's sudden demand for more oxygen is called

   a. myocardial ischemia.
   b. angina pectoris.
   c. congestive heart failure.
   d. none of these

3. Myocardial infarction, or heart attack, can be described as

   a. excess blood entering the heart.
   b. death, from oxygen deprivation, of a portion of the heart muscle.
   c. development of narrowing of the heart valves.
   d. any of these causes

4. Heart attack frequently is mistaken for "heartburn" by the patient.

   a. true   b. false

5. The symptoms of myocardial infarction are

   a. crushing chest pain.
   b. shortness of breath.
   c. nausea.
   d. sweating.
   e. all of these

6. If the heart stops, CPR may be very effective in starting it again.

   a. true   b. false

7. Some of the emotional concerns common after a myocardial infarction are

   a. depression.
   b. fear of another attack.
   c. fear that one's useful life will be over.
   d. sleepless nights.
   e. all of these

8. After a heart attack, moderate exercise helps develop _____, a system of smaller blood vessels providing alternative routes for blood.

   a. new arteries
   b. cardiac circulation
   c. collateral circulation
   d. none of these

9. The main function of the heart is

   a. as a pump.
   b. osmosis.
   c. filtration.
   d. none of these

10. _____ is an enzyme that binds to a blood clot and dissolves it.

   a. LDL
   b. HDL
   c. TPA
   d. CPR

11. Angioplasty is an operative procedure used to remove a clot blocking a blood vessel in a heart attack.

   a. true   b. false

12. Highly technical treatment for heart attack has removed the necessity for personal responsibility in practicing good health habits.

   a. true   b. false

13. Some health practices that decrease the risk of heart attack are all of these *except*

  a. maintaining an exercise program.
  b. eating less salt.
  c. eating plenty of red meat.
  d. stopping smoking.

14. Strokes, or cerebrovascular accidents, occur when one or more cerebral arteries become clogged or begin to hemorrhage.

  a. true   b. false

15. Most strokes are triggered by

  a. formation of clots in atherosclerotic cerebral arteries.
  b. a mass detached from a clot or fatty deposit elsewhere in the circulatory system traveling through the vessels and clogging a cerebral artery.
  c. a cerebral artery burst.
  d. all of these
  e. a and b only
  f. b and c only
  g. none of these

16. A common cause of cardiovascular problems in children and young adults is _____, a disease that can frequently be prevented through the use of _____.

  a. pertussis, aspirin
  b. rheumatic fever, antibiotics
  c. congenital heart defects, surgery
  d. congenital heart defects, antibiotics

17. Many of the congenital heart defects that used to be fatal can now be cured with surgery.

    a. true   b. false

Answer Key

1. a (p. 296)
2. b (p. 296)
3. b (p. 296)
4. a (p. 297)
5. e (pp. 297-298)
6. a (p. 298, Study Guide)
7. e (pp. 299-300, TV)
8. c (p. 300)
9. a (TV)
10. c (TV)
11. a (TV)
12. b (TV)
13. c (TV)
14. a (p. 300)
15. d (p. 300)
16. b (p. 304)
17. a (pp. 304-305)

LESSON 14   Heart Attack: How Can We Prevent It?

*To him who devotes his life to science, nothing can give more
happiness than increasing the number of his discoveries, but his
cup full of joy is full when the results of his studies immediately
find practical application.*

**Louis Pasteur
reprinted in *Human Development*, 2nd ed.**

Learning Objectives

Knowledge

Upon successful completion of all assignments in this lesson, you
should be able to

1. Identify several of the controllable risk factors for contracting a
    cardiovascular disease and discuss how they can be reduced.

2. Describe lifestyle behaviors that help maintain a healthy
    cardiovascular system.

3. Discuss the importance of evaluating a child's health to minimize
    the possibility of heart disease in adulthood.

4. Discuss some of the broad measures that can be undertaken to
    lessen the health risks of the population.

5. Explain the role of diet and exercise in improving cardiovascular
    health.

6. Describe some of the measures that can be taken to decrease smoking in the population.

Attitude

1. Discuss some of the aspects of your own heredity and lifestyle as they relate to your risk of heart disease.

Overview

In this lesson the Framingham Study is presented. This study has been extremely important in the understanding of cardiovascular disease and other health issues. The study has been repeated around the country with many different groups of people, each time deriving comparable results. Because of this study and the findings in similar studies, a great deal is known about the risk factors related to cardiovascular disease.

Nowhere is the lowering of risk factors more important than in the control of cardiovascular disease. The information in this lesson covers aspects of your lifestyle that you can control. Most of the material in this lesson has been discussed before, but it is significant enough to repeat.

Though it is important to know which of the uncontrollable risk factors apply to your own situation, it is not productive to be overly concerned about these. You have completed several types of self-appraisal exercises and now should have a fairly clear idea of your own risk factors. Concentrate on lowering the risks you can control. If you don't think you can manage trying to improve all your risk factors at once, work on one at a time until you have them all under control. It doesn't matter *where* you begin, but rather that you do begin!

Study Assignments

Textbook - Chapter 11, "Cardiovascular Health And Disease," pp. 305-311

TV - Program 14, "Heart Attack: How Can We Prevent It?"

Key Terms

controllable risk factors (p. 305)
uncontrollable risk factors (p. 305)

Text Focus Questions

1. What are the risk factors of heart disease that the individual can control? How does each influence the risk of heart disease?

2. What are the uncontrollable risk factors that have to be considered in evaluating an individual's risks?

3. How can an individual lower his/her risk of heart disease?

4. Why is it important to consider the effect of multiple risks in cardiovascular disease?

TV Focus Questions

1. What far-reaching knowledge has the Framingham Study provided?

2. Why is it important that the health of children be evaluated to lower the risk of heart disease in later life?

3. What broad actions can be taken to lower the health risks of the population?

4. What can parents do to start their children on a path to good cardiovascular health?

5. What diet and exercise habits are important to decrease the risk of heart disease?

6. What measures need to be taken regarding smoking in the population to decrease cardiovascular disease?

Optional Strengthening Exercise

1. Based on the results of self-assessments, assess your risks, and if indicated, plan a change in lifestyle to lower your chances of developing heart disease.

Self Test

1. Heredity and age can't be controlled, but risk factors that can be include

   a. improper diet.
   b. obesity.
   c. smoking.
   d. lack of exercise.
   e. stress.
   f. all of the above
   g. a, b, and c only
   h. b and d only

2. There is significant evidence that diets high in _____ are related to high serum cholesterol levels, a potentially dangerous risk factor for cardiovascular disease.

   a. saturated fats
   b. unsaturated fats
   c. complex carbohydrates

3. Lowering salt intake is really not very important in controlling high blood pressure.

   a. true   b. false

4. While the evidence linking obesity to coronary heart disease is unclear, there is no doubt that excess weight makes the heart work harder.

   a. true   b. false

5. In the Framingham Study the three risk factors mentioned most frequently in those who had heart attacks were _____, _____, and _____. This study is felt to be indicative of the population as a whole.

   a. high cholesterol, hypertension, smoking
   b. hypertension, smoking, exercise
   c. smoking, stress, high cholesterol
   d. stress, exercise, hypertension

6. Within ten years after they stop smoking, people who quit achieve about the same risk level of heart attack as nonsmokers.

   a. true   b. false

7. Regular aerobic exercise tends to

   a. lower blood pressure.
   b. reduce stress.
   c. help control obesity.
   d. all of these

8. It has been proven beyond any doubt that stress causes cardiovascular disease.

   a. true   b. false

9. One of the most troublesome aspects of cardiovascular disease risk factors is the way they tend to reinforce one another.

   a. true   b. false

10. The major way to maintain a healthy cardiovascular system is to

    a. stop smoking.
    b. begin a regular endurance exercise program.
    c. lower your fat intake.
    d. increase fruit and vegetable intake and lower sugar intake.
    e. lower salt intake.
    f. reduce alcohol intake.
    g. all of these
    h. none of these

Answer Key

1. f (pp. 306-307, TV)   6. a (p. 306)
2. a (p. 306, TV)   7. d (p. 307)
3. b (TV)   8. b (p. 307, TV)
4. a (p. 307)   9. a (p. 307)
5. a (TV)   10. g (p. 310, TV)

LESSON 15   Cancer: The Causes

"The absence of alternatives clears the mind marvelously."

Henry A. Kissinger

Learning Objectives

Knowledge

Upon successful completion of all assignments in this lesson, you should be able to

1. Explain what cancer is and identify various types of cancer.

2. Describe the process of metastasis.

3. Discuss some of the emotional, psychological, and social effects of cancer.

4. Discuss the nutritional factors thought to decrease the risks of cancer.

5. Describe the relationship between smoking and lung cancer.

6. Discuss the relative importance of cancer in the United States today.

Attitude

1. Examine your own attitudes toward cancer and determine whether they are realistic considering the knowledge you have gained in these lessons.

Overview

Though cancer is probably the most feared disease in America today, there is really much to feel hopeful about. There are large numbers of people alive and well who have been cured of cancer, medicine has progressed far in the search for cancer cures, and scientists have taught us much about lowering our risks of developing cancer.

The term cancer refers to a whole group of fairly mysterious diseases usually characterized by uncontrollable growth of cells. These cells can metastasize, or spread, to distant areas of the body, causing disease in both the original or primary site and elsewhere.

Modern lifestyles and industrialization have contributed to the high incidence of cancer in recent years. An incredible amount of cancer research has produced dramatic increases in knowledge about the causes, prevention, and treatment of cancer. As with other diseases, prevention and early detection are crucial in lowering the mortality rate of cancer.

The use of tobacco and certain other carcinogens has long been established as a significant risk factor in cancer. More recently, diet and other factors have been recognized to be equally hazardous. The next three lessons will discuss several aspects of cancer. Pay close attention to the SEVEN WARNING SIGNALS, early detection aids, and the prevention recommendations cited.

Study Assignments

Textbook - Chapter 12, "Cancer: Some Cause For Hope,"
pp. 313-318

TV - Program 15, "Cancer: The Causes"

Key Terms

cancer (p. 314)
malignant neoplasm (p. 314)
tissue (p. 315)
mitosis (p. 315, TV)
tumor (p. 315, TV)
neoplasm (p. 315, TV)
benign tumor (p. 315, TV)
malignant tumor (p. 315, TV)
metastases (p. 315, TV)
metastatic growth (p. 315)
carcinomas (p. 316)
epithelium (p. 316)
sarcomas (p. 316)
adenocarcinomas (p. 316)
lymphomas (p. 316)
leukemia (p. 316, TV)
melanomas (p. 316)
anaplastic (p. 316)

Text Focus Questions

1. What is cancer? What are the characteristics of cancer cells?

2. How important a health risk is cancer?

3. What are the differences between benign tumors and malignant tumors?

4. Explain the metastatic growth of cancer.

5. List and describe the most common types of cancer.

6. What are some of the psychological and social aspects of cancer? Why are these important?

TV Focus Questions

1. What are some of the general characteristics of cancer cells?

2. List some of the most important risk factors related to cancer.

3. How are certain nutritional factors thought to decrease the risks of cancer?

4. Discuss the relationship between smoking and lung cancer.

5. How does interferon work in the treatment of cancer?

Optional Strengthening Exercise

1. Evaluate your lifestyle habits, indicating positive choices that might prevent cancer and negative habits that would enhance your cancer risk factors.

Self Test

1. Fear is a very frustrating aspect of cancer prevention, detection, and treatment.

   a. true   b. false

2. Cancer is a group of more than 100 diseases characterized by the uncontrolled growth and spread of abnormal cells.

   a. true   b. false

3. Some characteristics of cancer cells are

   a. cell reproduction does not stop.
   b. cells form an abnormal growth.
   c. cells do not cooperate with one another.
   d. all of the above
   e. a and b only
   f. c and d only

4. All tumors are malignant.

   a. true   b. false

5. Benign tumors

   a. are usually not life-threatening.
   b. will not usually recur once removed.
   c. may cause problems because of their size or position.
   d. usually metastasize.
   e. all of these
   f. all except d

6. Because of _____, early detection is the crucial factor in cancer survival rates.

   a. neoplasms
   b. metastasis
   c. malignancy
   d. leukemia

7. Carcinomas arise in the

   a. epithelium.
   b. connective tissue.
   c. nerve tissue.
   d. blood-forming tissues.

8. _____ are those cancers whose cellular structure is so abnormal that they no longer resemble the cells of the tissue from which they originated.

   a. Neoplasms
   b. Sarcomas
   c. Anaplastic cancers
   d. Lymphomas

9. _____ kills more Americans than do other cancers.

   a. Colon cancer
   b. Breast cancer
   c. Lung cancer
   d. Bone cancer

10. Though cancer is a very serious disease, with modern treatment it has minimal psychological effect on the family.

   a. true   b. false

11. _____, cancer of the blood-forming tissues such as bone marrow, frequently strikes children.

   a. Lymphoma
   b. Leukemia
   c. Sarcoma
   d. Hodgkins disease

12. Tobacco is one of the main carcinogens.

   a. true   b. false

13. Many cancer patients face problems maintaining adequate health insurance, especially if they are not covered by group policies.

   a. true   b. false

14. More recent cancer research has focused on the effects of diet on cancer.

   a. true   b. false

15. The treatment of cancer usually involves

   a. surgery.
   b. X-rays.
   c. chemotherapy.
   d. interferon.
   e. a combination of the above

155

Answer Key

1. a (p. 313)
2. a (p. 314)
3. d (p. 315, TV)
4. b (p. 315)
5. f (p. 315)
6. b (p. 315, TV)
7. a (p. 316)
8. c (p. 316)
9. c (TV)
10. b (p. 317)
11. b (TV)
12. a (TV)
13. a (p. 318)
14. a (TV)
15. e (TV)

LESSON 16   Cancer: How To Detect And Prevent It

"Fry Now -- Pay Later"

On a billboard featuring a sunbather
American Cancer Society

Learning Objectives

Knowledge

Upon successful completion of all assignments in this lesson, you should be able to

1. Identify and discuss several risk factors associated with cancer.

2. Explain the importance of early detection of cancer and describe procedures and recommendations for self-examination and early diagnosis.

3. List cancer's "Seven Warning Signals" and explain their significance.

4. Explain the procedures for breast self-examination and for testicular self-examination.

5. Discuss the steps most important in surviving cancer.

Attitude

1. List the lifestyle modifications you can make to reduce your risk of cancer.

2. Begin (or continue) a program of breast self-examination or testicular self-examination.

Overview

In the previous lesson on cancer, the terms *prevention* and *early detection* are mentioned several times as being the most critical factors in surviving cancer. This may seem to be an oversimplification of a serious health threat, but the truth is this: the chances for survival decrease if the malignancy is not detected early, no matter what treatment is used later. Further, there are lifestyle behaviors (such as smoking) that significantly increase the risks of developing cancer.

Not all cancers can be prevented (even with a healthy lifestyle), but a combination of lowering risk factors and heeding the Seven Warning Signals outlined by the American Cancer Society can certainly better your odds. Nowhere is sharing knowledge and taking responsibility for lifestyle behaviors more important than in the area of cancer.

Early detection techniques should be learned and adopted as a regular activity in your daily routine. Particularly important to women are monthly breast self-examinations and regular pap smears. Both of these measures are directed at the early detection of cancers that are very treatable if diagnosed promptly. Likewise for men, testicular self-examinations and regular medical checkups of the prostate gland greatly enhance the chance for early treatment and cure of these cancers.

If you smoke, you should be convinced by this time that you must stop. Cigarette smoking is the major risk factor for virtually every disease of the lungs or heart. Remember, once it begins, lung cancer carries a very high death rate, no matter what the treatment. The risks to which you expose those around you cannot be denied either.

The most important lesson this unit should teach you is to pay attention to your body. Practice good habits and don't ignore any unusual signs or symptoms. Chances are those symptoms are not cancer, but if they are, early diagnosis improves your chances of recovery.

Study Assignments

Textbook - Chapter 12, "Cancer: Some Cause For Hope," pp. 318-326

TV - Program 16, "Cancer: How To Detect And Prevent It"

Key Terms

carcinogenic (p. 320)
mammography (TV)

Text Focus Questions

1. How does heredity affect risk factors for cancer?

2. What are some of the most important environmental risk factors for cancer?

3. In what ways do tobacco and alcohol increase the risk of cancer?

4. List and describe the importance of risk factors other than tobacco and alcohol.

5. Why are the Seven Warning Signals important in the detection and treatment of cancer?

6. What are some of the other precautions that can be taken to ensure early detection if a cancer exists?

7. How do delay and denial affect the chance of cancer being cured?

TV Focus Questions

1. What are some of the cancer risk factors other than cigarette smoking and diet?

2. What are the Seven Warning Signals of cancer? (You should remember these from the previous lesson.)

3. Describe the procedure for breast self-examination.

4. What two steps are the most important in surviving cancer?

Optional Strengthening Exercise

1. Visit the American Cancer Society and find out what services it offers cancer patients, their families, and the general public.

Self Test

1. Heredity is interesting but plays no part in the prevention and early detection of cancer.

    a. true   b. false

2. Evidence linking cancer to high-dose, long-term exposure to various workplace chemicals has been quite conclusive.

    a. true   b. false

3. _____ is a very dangerous risk factor for developing cancer.

    a. Poor diet
    b. Herpes infection
    c. Cigarette smoking
    d. Lack of exercise

4. Cigarette smoking is a major risk factor for developing

    a. lung cancer.
    b. oral cavity cancer.
    c. cancer of the cervix.
    d. none of the above
    e. a and b only
    f. b and c only
    g. a and c only

161

5. A woman should examine her breasts

    a. once a week.
    b. once a month.
    c. twice a year.
    d. once a year.

6. Generally, breast self-examination is a systematic means for a woman to detect a lump or thickening in her breasts.

    a. true   b. false

7. The first sign of testicular cancer is usually a slight lump in one of the testes and any change in its feel.

    a. true   b. false

8. _____ can be an early sign of colon/rectal cancer.

    a. Nausea
    b. Loss of appetite
    c. An obvious lump in the abdomen
    d. Blood in the stool

9. Persons with fair-skinned pigmentation are less susceptible to skin cancer than those of darker pigmentation.

    a. true   b. false

10. _____ and _____ are the most important steps in surviving cancer.

    a. Surgery, chemotherapy
    b. Prevention, early detection
    c. Chemotherapy, X-ray

Answer Key

1. b (pp. 318-319)
2. a (p. 320)
3. c (p. 320)
4. e (p. 320)
5. b (pp. 323-324, TV)
6. a (TV)
7. a (p. 324)
8. d (p. 325, TV)
9. b (TV)
10. b (TV, also throughout chapter)

LESSON 17   Cancer Treatment: Success Story In The Making

"The only way of discovering the limits of the possible is to venture a little way past them into the impossible."

Arthur C. Clarke, *Profiles of the Future*

Learning Objectives

Knowledge

Upon successful completion of all assignments in this lesson, you should be able to

1. Define the procedure known as staging and explain its importance in determining an appropriate treatment.

2. Identify and discuss the primary treatments available for dealing with cancer and the dangerous appeal of quack remedies for the disease.

3. Describe some new developments in treatment and diagnosis that offer hope for cancer patients.

4. Discuss the symptoms, treatment, and outlook for the person with leukemia.

5. Compare the treatment of cancer in children with the treatment in adults.

6. Discuss some of the ways in which people attempt to cope with cancer and explain how cancer patients can be helped to deal with the disease.

7. Explain the necessity of educating the cancer patient and his/her family.

Attitude

1. Discuss an experience you or a family member may have had with cancer, from both the physical and the emotional perspectives.

Overview

Through research and modern advances in medicine, the outlook for cancer patients has improved dramatically in recent years. In fact Dr. Vincent DeVita, a Director of the National Cancer Institute, has called cancer "one of the most curable of the chronic diseases." Three major techniques are used in treatment: surgery, radiation, chemotherapy, or -- more often -- a combination of these.

A good example of the progress being made in cancer treatment is in the treatment of lymphocytic leukemia, a fairly common malignancy in children. Not long ago almost all children stricken with this disease died within a year or so. Now, with early effective treatment a very significant number survive and never have a relapse.

Along with the treatment of the physical aspects of cancer, psychological support is extraordinarily important to the patient's outlook for being cured. So often the diagnosis brings an overwhelming sense of hopelessness, helplessness, and impending doom. This attitude must be overcome and the patient mobilized to help fight his/her own disease if successful treatment is to be accomplished. The patient, the family, the doctor, and the medical team must be equal partners in the treatment of cancer. This partnership in treatment is important in any serious disease process, but nowhere is it more crucial than in the treatment of cancer.

As the lessons about cancer have unfolded, you have learned much about the importance of research, prevention, and early detection of cancer. Now you learn the importance of effective treatment. These four components -- research, prevention, early detection, and effective treatment -- have given hundreds of thousands of people a cure for cancer. They are living proof that there is hope, that cancer is curable.

Study Assignments

Textbook - Chapter 12, "Cancer: Some Cause For Hope," pp. 326-334

TV - Program 17, "Cancer Treatment: A Success Story In The Making"

Key Terms

radiation therapy (p. 328, TV)
chemotherapy (p. 328, TV)
oncologist (TV)
leukemia (TV)
remission (TV)

Text Focus Questions

1. How is surgery used in the treatment of cancer? In what cancers is it most useful?

2. How does radiation therapy work to cure cancer?

3. Give examples of some of the drugs used in chemotherapy and tell which cancers they are used with.

4. What are some of the dangers of quackery in the treatment of cancer?

5. What are some of the difficulties that patients encounter in coping with cancer? List some options available to help families coping with cancer.

TV Focus Questions

1. What are the symptoms of acute lymphocytic leukemia? How is it treated?

2. How does the treatment of cancer in children usually differ from the treatment of cancer in adults?

3. How has the treatment of leukemia progressed over recent years?

4. What emotional support factors are important in working with cancer patients and their families?

Optional Strengthening Exercise

1. Talk with a cured or recovering cancer patient or a health care worker and identify the problems a person may encounter and have to cope with when "living with cancer."

Self Test

1. The basic goals for cancer treatment include

   a. cure.
   b. prolongation of life.
   c. control of symptoms.
   d. all of these
   e. a and b only

2. After cancer has been detected, physicians use a procedure known as staging to assess and plan treatment options.

   a. true   b. false

3. Surgery has proved to be particularly effective in the treatment of the following cancers *except*

   a. colon.
   b. stomach.
   c. blood cell.
   d. skin.

4. Radiation is rarely used in conjunction with surgery in cancer treatment because it is too dangerous.

   a. true   b. false

5. In recent years chemotherapy has become the major weapon against

   a. skin cancers.
   b. benign tumors.
   c. cancers of the stomach.
   d. cancers that have metastasized.

169

6. _____, an immune modifier manufactured naturally by the body, works through direct action on the cells or through its effect on the immune system.

    a. Erythromycin
    b. Nitrogen mustard
    c. Interferon
    d. Rifampin

7. Some authorities consider cancer one of the most curable chronic diseases.

    a. true   b. false

8. Some of the more common symptoms of leukemia are

    a. pallor and fatigue.
    b. bruising and nosebleeds.
    c. an increased number of infections.
    d. all of these

9. The treatment of children with cancers usually involves _____ radiation and _____ chemotherapy.

    a. less, more
    b. more, less
    c. less, less
    d. more, more

10. In cancer treatment it is very important that the host be mobilized to fight the cancer.

    a. true   b. false

11. Some of the advantages of chemotherapy in treating cancer are that

   a. it can be given at home or on an outpatient basis.
   b. it does no damage to cells.
   c. side effects are usually short term.
   d. there are no side effects.
   e. all of these
   f. a and c only

12. Some important aspects in the emotional support for patients with cancer include

   a. giving hope, not isolation.
   b. the patient understanding the reason for treatment.
   c. family and patient being partners in the treatment.
   d. never lying to the patient.
   e. the patient playing an active role in treatment.
   f. the patient never being told he/she has cancer.
   g. all except e
   h. all except f
   i. all except d

13. In order for the patient to take an active role in the treatment process, he/she must be educated about the disease and treatment.

   a. true   b. false

14. Since medicine has advanced so much, there is little reason to do much more research in the area of cancer.

   a. true   b. false

15. The greatest danger of quackery is that the patient may delay getting appropriate treatment and lessen his/her chances for survival.

    a. true   b. false

Answer Key

 1. d (p. 326)
 2. a (p. 326)
 3. c (p. 326)
 4. b (p. 328)
 5. d (p. 328)
 6. c (p. 329)
 7. a (TV)
 8. d (TV)
 9. a (TV)
10. a (TV)
11. f (TV)
12. h (pp. 332-333, TV)
13. a (p. 333, TV)
14. b (TV)
15. a (p. 331)

LESSON 18   Street Drugs And Medicine Chests

We are walking around with myriad combinations of tranquilizers, cough medicines and headache remedies in our systems. It's sanctioned by society, it's legal -- and it's very, very dangerous.

**Richard Hughes and Robert Brewin,
"The Daze of Our Lives," reprinted
in Charles Carroll's** *Drugs in Modern Society*

Learning Objectives

Knowledge

Upon successful completion of all assignments in this lesson, you should be able to

1. Explain what drugs are, why people use them, and how drug addiction can develop.

2. Describe patterns of drug use and explain the relevance of the agent-host-environment model to drug dependence.

3. Summarize the main effects of drugs, describe the different ways in which drugs are administered, and discuss the relationship between methods of administration and effects.

4. List, describe, and give examples of the main types of drugs, including sedatives/hypnotics, stimulants (including cocaine), marijuana, volatile solvents, opiate narcotics, and psychedelics/hallucinogens.

5. Discuss programs that help drug abusers and efforts at the societal level to combat the drug problem.

6. Discuss reasons that adolescents seem particularly prone to drug use.

7. Explain the particular risks in cocaine use.

8. Discuss three factors in preventing drug use in adolescents.

Attitude

1. Compare and contrast your attitudes toward alcohol and other drug use.

2. Examine your own use, if any, of drugs, including caffeine and nicotine (even sugar if you use it to excess).

Overview

Americans are definitely a drug-oriented people. Whenever we feel a small pain anywhere in the body, find ourselves under stress, or just want to feel good, we think of taking a pill first and only later consider other and healthier alternatives. While alarmed and indignant when adolescents use street drugs, many never acknowledge that their own consumption of alcohol, tobacco, and tranquilizers gives children a model for drug use. It is important for you to analyze your own relationship with drugs as you complete this lesson.

It is vital to understand the body's reactions to and greatest dangers from the major classifications of psychoactive drugs. Depressants are the most used and abused due to their calming effects and relief of pain. The major dangers associated with depressants are the potential for developing a dependency and a tolerance that results from using them on a regular basis. The greatest risk to the user comes from combining two or more depressant drugs. Many people die each year from these combinations.

Stimulants are used as a means to stay awake, to diet, to provide an imagined increase in performance level, or to experience the euphoric rush they provide. Stimulants increase blood pressure and heart action, mask fatigue, and create a psychological dependency, making them particularly dangerous.

Hallucinogens are taken, illegally, for their mind-altering effects. None are routinely prescribed for any medical condition. The greatest dangers from hallucinogens are their unpredictability, the high incidence of accidents, and the psychotic episodes caused by illusions and hallucinations.

Inhalants, sometimes the only psychoactive substance available to younger children, can cause brain damage and occasionally death. They are becoming more controlled, but many substances containing toxic chemicals are still readily obtained in any grocery or drug store.

Marijuana deserves special mention. In past years many persons, especially the youth, were told half-truths, untruths, and exaggerations about the drug. Then the pendulum swung the other way and marijuana was depicted as a fairly benign drug whose major danger was the fact that it was illegal. Current research paints a more accurate picture that lies somewhere between the two extremes. It's a fact that there is a decrease in brain function with chronic marijuana use; short-term memory, math skills, and reasoning are commonly affected. The latest information from the American Thoracic Society shows that chronic marijuana use results in similar long-term effects, as does cigarette smoking -- only more severe and sooner!

Overcoming drug problems is tough, but the concept is simple -- get your life in order and stop taking the drugs. Achieving this goal is extraordinarily difficult and requires much support from family, friends, and professionals. This help is available in most communities to those who ask for it. Well-known personalities who have publicly shared their problems have given hope to others seeking help.

It is important for parents, teachers, and other adults to serve as positive role models and to keep the lines of communication open for young people.

Study Assignments

Textbook - Chapter 13, "Drug Use And Abuse," pp. 337-369

TV - Program 18, "Street Drugs And Medicine Chests"

Key Terms

drug (p. 338)
psychoactive drugs (p. 338)
nonpsychoactive drugs (p. 338)
tolerance (p. 339)
dependence (p. 339)
withdrawal syndrome (p. 340)
addiction (p. 340)
receptor sites (p. 343)
side effects (p. 345)
teratogenic (p. 346)
allergy (p. 346)
anaphylactic shock (p. 346)
cross-sensitivity (p. 346)

methadone (p. 366)
peer pressure (TV)
OTC (over-the-counter) drug (TV)

Text Focus Questions

1. What are drugs? What is appropriate use of drugs?

2. Why do people use drugs?

3. Explain drug tolerance, dependence, and addiction.

4. How does the agent-host-environment model apply to drug use?

5. How do drugs interact with body cells?

6. Describe the various routes of administration of drugs. Why is each selected?

7. Explain the time-response and the dose-response relationships.

8. List and describe the effect of the various types of psychoactive drugs. What are the risks of each? Include sedatives/hypnotics, stimulants, marijuana, volatile solvents, opiate narcotics, and psychedelics/hallucinogens.

9. What are some of the options available in drug treatment?

10. How is society attempting to deal with drug abuse?

TV Focus Questions

1. Why are teenagers at great risk from drug problems?

2. What are the most common reasons that adults misuse and abuse drugs?

3. What are the particular risks associated with cocaine use?

4. What are some of the effects of sustained marijuana use on the brain?

5. What are some of the difficulties associated with treating and recovering from drug problems?

6. What are some of the most important things that parents and other adults can do to prevent youngsters from using drugs?

Optional Strengthening Exercises

1. Visit and get information about a therapeutic community approach to drug treatment.

2. Compile a list of resources for people with drug problems in your community.

3. Interview someone who has conquered a drug problem. Ask about his/her drug use, difficulties in recovery, etc.

Self Test

1. People use drugs to

    a. escape boredom.
    b. relieve pain and discomfort.
    c. relieve stress and tension.
    d. improve performance.
    e. all of these

2. Drugs are defined as

    a. illegal substances abused frequently by people.
    b. psychoactive substances that change a person's mood.
    c. substances that alter physical or mental functions when taken into the body.
    d. substances taken internally to cure some illness or injury.

3. Responsible drug use can include the use of drugs to do the following *except*

    a. relieve symptoms.
    b. improve performance.
    c. prevent illness.
    d. control chronic conditions.
    e. treat diseases.

4. _____ means that the body becomes adapted to the drug so that increasingly larger dosages are needed to produce the desired effect.

    a. Addiction
    b. Sensitivity
    c. Dependence
    d. Tolerance

5. _____ use of drugs means that the individual is using drugs to experience the effects that he/she considers beneficial to a particular situation and at this point the individual is at considerable risk of dependence.

    a. Experimental
    b. Recreational
    c. Situational
    d. Intensified

6. Peer pressure, family patterns, and cultural mores are some of the _____ factors in the agent-host-environmental model of drug use.

    a. agent
    b. host
    c. environment
    d. all of these

7. When an individual is dependent on a drug and its use is stopped suddenly, a serious reaction called withdrawal syndrome can occur.

    a. true   b. false

8. Side effects are mild, unexpected reactions to drugs.

    a. true   b. false

9. The drug's route of administration can be a crucial factor in its effect.

    a. true   b. false

10. It is important to remember that drugs can be excreted into breast milk and affect the nursing infant.

    a. true   b. false

11. When drugs taken together produce different or more extreme pharmacological actions than they would individually, the result is called

    a. tolerance.
    b. potentiation.
    c. inhibition.
    d. withdrawal syndrome.

12. Barbiturates are examples of

    a. major tranquilizers that are depressants.
    b. narcotics that are stimulants.
    c. sedative-hypnotics that are depressants.
    d. sedative-hypnotics that are hallucinogens.

13. Barbiturates are frequently associated with dependence and abuse because they induce

    a. synergism.
    b. dependence.
    c. sleep.
    d. hypnosis.

14. Death is frequently caused by combining _____ and alcohol.

    a. stimulants
    b. LSD
    c. barbiturates
    d. none of these

15. Drugs that are considered stimulants include all *except*

    a. caffeine.
    b. cocaine.
    c. amphetamines such as dexedrine.
    d. marijuana.

16. In large doses or over prolonged periods, amphetamines have unpredictable effects.

    a. true   b. false

17. _____ is the illicit drug that currently poses the greatest threat to public health in the United States.

    a. Methamphetamine
    b. PCP
    c. Cocaine
    d. Amyl nitrate

18. Marijuana affects the respiratory system as well as the brain.

    a. true   b. false

19. Smoking a joint every evening to unwind after a stressful day is certainly not drug abuse.

    a. true   b. false

20. Opiate narcotics are central nervous system depressants whose potential for dependence is great.

    a. true   b. false

21. LSD and PCP are examples of _____, whose effects _____ and are _____.

    a. hallucinogens, cause illusions, unpredictable
    b. stimulants, reduce psychotic symptoms, predictable
    c. hallucinogens, act as calming agents, unpredictable
    d. depressants, reduce pain, predictable

22. A major danger of the hallucinogenic drugs is their unpredictability and the possibility of a "bad" trip.

    a. true   b. false

23. Drug treatment groups based on the model of Alcoholics Anonymous are called

    a. methadone maintenance programs.
    b. individual therapy sessions.
    c. self-help groups.
    d. family therapy centers.

24. Drug users with a serious dependence are more likely to be treated on an out-patient basis.

    a. true   b. false

25. Stress-reducing methods and exercise can offer an alternative to drug use.

    a. true   b. false

26. Psychotherapy and counseling are of little use in the treatment of drug dependence.

    a. true   b. false

27. Society's approach to the control of drug use must be a multifaceted one.

    a. true   b. false

28. Teens are especially at risk of using drugs because of their problems with self-esteem and lack of social skills.

    a. true   b. false

29. Adults usually use drugs simply for recreation and enjoyment.

    a. true   b. false

30. Families feel the effects of a family member's drug problems through

    a. acute crisis with the drugs.
    b. isolation.
    c. conflicts.
    d. all of these

31. Parents who drink alcohol or take prescription drugs in excess really have little impact on their children.

    a. true   b. false

32. Recovery from drug problems may be simple in concept but is certainly not easy to accomplish.

    a. true   b. false

Answer Key

1. e (pp. 337-338)
2. c (p. 338)
3. b (p. 339)
4. d (p. 339)
5. d (p. 341)
6. c (p. 342)
7. a (p. 340)
8. b (p. 345)
9. a (p. 346)
10. a (p. 348)
11. b (p. 349)
12. c (p. 352)
13. b (p. 353)
14. c (p. 353)
15. d (p. 356)
16. a (p. 357)
17. c (p. 359)
18. a (p. 361, TV)
19. b (p. 361)
20. a (p. 363)
21. a (p. 364)
22. a (p. 364)
23. c (p. 366)
24. b (p. 366)
25. a (p. 366)
26. b (p. 366)
27. a (p. 367)
28. a (TV)
29. b (TV)
30. d (TV)
31. b (TV)
32. a (TV)

LESSON 19   Someone You Know Drinks Too Much

"To think...I was so glad my son only drank a little too much sometimes...he never used drugs..."

**The mother of a teenager who died in an
alcohol-related automobile accident**

Learning Objectives

Knowledge

Upon successful completion of all assignments in this lesson, you should be able to

1. Explain alcohol's effects on the body and the factors that lead to alcohol dependence.

2. Identify different types of destructive behavior associated with alcohol.

3. Describe alcoholism, listing progressive steps in its development and identifying some of the signs that indicate its presence.

4. Discuss some of the major health consequences of alcohol abuse.

5. Indicate the ways that you can guard against the development of alcoholism and the types of treatment that are available for those who are already problem drinkers.

6. Discuss the effective means to force an individual to face his/her alcohol problems.

7. List the key ingredients of treatment that achieve the greatest recovery rate.

Attitude

1. Explain your feelings about the implications of withholding highway funds from states where the legal drinking age is below 21.

2. Define responsible drinking.

3. Evaluate your relationship with alcohol, taking into consideration 1) the type and amount of beverage you consume, 2) the frequency of your consumption, 3) the conditions under which you drink, and 4) and your responsibility for your drinking practices.

Overview

The parent who says, "I am so glad my son/daughter doesn't use drugs; he/she just drinks" is missing the point that alcohol *is* a drug, the most abused of all drugs. More people are impaired or killed by the effects of alcohol than by any other drug. The fact that alcohol consumption is legal blinds many to the magnitude of the alcohol problem in this country.

When you consider that 1 person in 10 experiences major alcohol problems, you realize that you must know several of these people. The other 9 either never drink at all or will never encounter problems unless they drink irresponsibly. This lesson helps you to identify and understand problem drinkers and further demonstrates the general effects of alcohol on the body. Most important, you will learn the components of responsible drinking.

188

Alcohol is indeed a part of the "American way of life." We use alcohol for many reasons, but the bottom line is we want to feel differently. We drink alcohol for its effect. If you keep this simple explanation in mind and use good judgment, the first step toward responsible drinking already has been taken. It is important to know how much alcohol actually is being consumed and to clearly understand the effects of alcohol on vital organs.

Each individual must make a definite decision not to endanger the lives of others by drinking and driving. It is sad enough to destroy oneself with alcohol, but the greater tragedy is when innocent persons suffer because of the irresponsible drinking behavior of others.

There is hope for alcohol abusers and their families through a variety of options for treatment. Both a firm support system and a treatment program, consisting of several components, increase the alcoholic's level of commitment and in turn his/her chances of recovery. Obviously, the most important key to all of this is prevention. By learning to cope with the stresses of life in healthy ways, practicing responsible drinking habits, and never drinking alcohol when driving, most of the problems related to alcohol can be prevented. For your own safety and that of others, be part of the solution, not part of the problem.

Study Assignments

Textbook - Chapter 14, "Alcohol," pp. 371-387

TV - Program 19, "Someone You Know Drinks Too Much"

Key Terms

ethyl alcohol (p. 373)
blood alcohol level (BAL) (p. 373, TV)
pancreatitis (p. 379)

cirrhosis of the liver (p. 380)
alcoholic hepatitis (p. 381)
detoxification (p. 385)
alcoholic (TV)
Alcoholics Anonymous (TV)
tolerance (TV)
depressant (TV)
psychological dependence (TV)
physical dependence (TV)
proof (TV)

Text Focus Questions

1. How does alcohol affect the body?

2. What influence do physiological, psychological, and social factors have on alcohol use?

3. How does alcohol use affect behavior in destructive ways?

4. Explain the alcohol continuum.

5. What are the signs of alcoholism?

6. How prevalent is alcoholism in America? Include discussion of particular ethnic/religious groups in this.

7. How are some of the systems of the body particularly affected by alcohol?

8. How can one use alcohol responsibly?

9. What are some of the more successful types of treatment programs for alcohol abuse?

TV Focus Questions

1. What percentage of people experience major alcohol problems?

2. What are some of the reasons for drinking?

3. List the types of problems that alcoholics experience.

4. What influential factors cause people to have alcohol problems?

5. What are the most effective means to force an individual to face his/her alcohol problem?

6. List the key ingredients of treatment that achieve the greatest recovery rate.

7. What are some things individuals can do to keep the risk of alcohol problems to a minimum?

Optional Strengthening Exercises

1. Through research or interviews, describe a residential treatment program for individuals who abuse alcohol.

2. Contact a local Alcoholics Anonymous chapter and attend an "open" meeting if this is possible, or interview a recovering alcoholic who will discuss his/her problems and recovery with you.

3. Explore your own alcohol use. If alcohol is creating problems in your life, get help! At least discuss your use of alcohol with a counselor at the college where you registered.

Self Test

1. Alcohol use in the United States is actually decreasing while the use of other drugs is increasing.

    a. true   b. false

2. Alcohol is absorbed _____ from the stomach and small intestine into the bloodstream.

    a. rapidly
    b. slowly

3. The following are all factors influencing alcohol absorption *except*

    a. drinking history.
    b. the drinker's body weight.
    c. drinking rate.
    d. the drinker's emotional state.
    e. the type of alcohol consumed.

4. Alcohol is a powerful

    a. stimulant.
    b. psychedelic.
    c. mood elevator.
    d. depressant.

5. The phenomenon in which an individual has to drink more and more to get the desired effect is

    a. depression.
    b. psychological dependence.
    c. tolerance.
    d. physical dependence.

6. Individuals who drink too much frequently experience

   a. problems with interpersonal relationships.
   b. work-related problems.
   c. increased incidence of accidents.
   d. all of the above

7. An individual with a blood alcohol level of 0.05 percent is generally considered drunk.

   a. true   b. false

8. Most occasional drinkers are in danger of developing more serious drinking problems.

   a. true   b. false

9. The "excessive drinker" experiences frequent episodes of uncontrollable drinking affecting work, family, and social relationships.

   a. true   b. false

10. Some of the changes in behavior that warn of alcoholism are all of these *except*

    a. secretive drinking.
    b. repeated, conscious attempts at abstinence.
    c. drinking "hard" liquor.
    d. having five or more drinks daily.
    e. having two or more blackouts while drinking.

11. An individual's family history may have little to do with that person's use of alcohol.

   a. true   b. false

12. The health problems most frequently linked to alcohol abuse are

   a. gastrointestinal disorders and malnutrition.
   b. liver damage and glandular disorders.
   c. central nervous system and cardiovascular disorders.
   d. a and b
   e. all of these

13. The effect of the mother's alcohol use on the unborn child may occur very early in the pregnancy, even if the mother consumes low doses.

   a. true   b. false

14. An occasional abuse of alcohol is not dangerous if you are not dependent on alcohol.

   a. true   b. false

15. Detoxification and counseling can be very useful over the longer term to help the person deal with the underlying problems causing the alcoholism.

   a. true   b. false

16. The _____ program, one of the most successful treatment programs, has the members begin by admitting they have lost control over alcohol.

    a. Mothers Against Drunk Drivers
    b. Palmer Drug Abuse Program
    c. Alcoholics Anonymous
    d. none of the above

17. You "burn off" approximately _____ drink(s) per hour, no matter what your size.

    a. 3
    b. 1
    c. 2
    d. 4

18. Heavy drinking shortens your life.

    a. true   b. false

19. The incidence of persons with major alcohol problems is approximately 1 in 10.

    a. true   b. false

20. Some of the characteristics of alcoholism are that

    a. cultural attitudes influence its incidence, stress contributes to it, and it is limited to low socioeconomic groups.
    b. it runs in families, stress contributes to it, and it is limited to low socioeconomic groups.
    c. it runs in families, cultural attitudes influence its incidence, and it is limited to low socioeconomic groups.
    d. it runs in families, cultural attitudes influence its incidence, and stress contributes to it.

21. The liver detoxifies approximately _____ percent of the alcohol absorbed.

    a. 50
    b. 100
    c. 90
    d. 20

22. The most important component(s) of responsible drinking is/are

    a. to exercise good judgment.
    b. to never mix drinking and driving.
    c. to never use alcohol as an escape.
    d. to never drink every day.
    e. to drink intermittently for no more than 1/2 hour to 1 hour, then stop.
    f. all of these

Answer Key

1. b (p. 371)
2. a (p. 372)
3. e (p. 373)
4. d (p. 373, TV)
5. c (p. 374, TV)
6. d (p. 375, TV)
7. b (p. 375, TV)
8. b (p. 377)
9. a (p. 377)
10. c (p. 378)
11. a (p. 378)
12. e (p. 379)
13. a (p. 382, TV)
14. b (p. 384)
15. a (p. 385)
16. c (p. 385)
17. b (TV)
18. a (TV)
19. a (TV)
20. d (TV)
21. c (TV)
22. f (TV)

LESSON 20   Smoking...Hazardous To Your Health

"Smoking is guilty of being the leading preventable cause of disease and death in this country."

C. Everett Koop, M.D., Former Surgeon General, U.S. Public Health Service

Learning Objectives

Knowledge

Upon successful completion of all assignments in this lesson, you should be able to

1. Analyze the current smoking trends in the United States.

2. Describe in detail the effects of cigarette smoke on the body.

3. Describe the role smoking plays in increasing the risk of coronary heart disease, cancer, bronchitis, and emphysema.

4. Discuss the dangers of tobacco use during pregnancy.

5. Name the major voluntary health agencies active in research concerning the effects of smoking.

6. Discuss the contradictory role the U.S. government plays in the production and consumption of tobacco.

7. Describe the effects of passive smoking (being in the presence of others' tobacco smoke).

Attitude

1. If you smoke -- STOP!

2. Support the efforts of the American Lung Association, American Cancer Society, and American Heart Association in their efforts to reduce the incidence of smoking.

3. Analyze your reactions to the nonsmokers' rights movement.

Overview

There remains no doubt that tobacco use is the greatest health risk in our country today. Of most concern is the increase in the number of young women who are beginning to smoke in spite of all the known dangers of smoking. The increased use of smokeless tobacco among teenagers and young adult males is also a major concern for health experts. Tobacco companies spend millions of dollars every year trying to convince us that smoking and chewing are glamorous, macho, or the "in" thing to do. The "big three" voluntary health agencies -- the American Lung Association, American Cancer Society, and American Heart Association -- have banded together into the Tri-Agency Coalition to counter the tobacco industry's claims and to educate people to the truth about tobacco use. Amazingly, even with all this information people are still smoking.

The consequences of tobacco use are well-known and immediate in their effect on the body. Somehow, it's always mistakenly assumed that smoking affects only persons who have smoked for many years. Carbon monoxide, one of the gases released in smoking (and in automobile exhaust), immediately reduces the oxygen-carrying capacity of the blood in every smoker. Carbon monoxide may not be as familiar to the public as nicotine or tar, but it is just as damaging. Tobacco also has an adverse effect on the heart and lungs.

Since the surgeon general's first report on smoking and health in 1964, cigarette smoking among adults has decreased. Unfortunately, it has not stopped completely, and in fact, lung cancer in women has increased dramatically. This phenomenon is a sign that women are not heeding the clear warning and are continuing to smoke. Teenagers are also beginning to smoke at an alarming rate.

The effects of tobacco smoke on the nonsmoker also have come to the forefront. The nonsmoker, in close quarters, is exposed to the same toxic chemicals as the smoker. In an effort to protect themselves against secondhand smoke and to improve the health of their communities, citizens have pressed to have nonsmoking ordinances passed. This ground swell has moved across the country and spread to state legislatures. Again, voluntary health agencies, such as the American Lung Association, have provided leadership in this effort to improve the health of all people.

Study Assignments

Textbook - Chapter 15, "Tobacco," pp. 389-397

TV - Program 20, "Smoking...Hazardous To Your Health"

Key Terms

nicotine (p. 391)
carbon monoxide (p. 392)
tar (p. 392)
benzopyrene (p. 392)
passive smoking (p. 397, TV)
chronic obstructive pulmonary disease (COPD) (TV)
American Lung Association (TV)
American Heart Association (TV)
American Cancer Society (TV)

Text Focus Questions

1. What are the smoking trends in the U.S. today?

2. What are the effects of tobacco use on the body?

3. What are some of the long-term effects of cigarette smoking?

4. List and describe the progression of bronchitis to emphysema.

5. Explain the role of smoking in contributing to the risk of cancer.

6. Describe the relationship between smoking and coronary heart disease.

7. Why is it dangerous for the pregnant woman to smoke?

8. How does passive smoking affect the nonsmoker?

TV Focus Questions

1. How prevalent are the problems of smoking in the U.S.?

2. Describe some of the effects of smoking on lung function and disease.

3. What has the Framingham Study shown about the risks of smoking?

4. What specific risks to the unborn child are associated with the mother's smoking?

5. What do we know about the effects of passive smoking and sidestream (secondhand) smoke?

6. What are the addicting properties of tobacco?

7. Is there a safe cigarette? Explain.

8. What contradictory role does the U.S. government play in the production and consumption of tobacco?

9. What voluntary health agencies are taking a leading role in reducing the incidence of cigarette smoking?

Optional Strengthening Exercises

1. Visit the American Lung Association, American Heart Association, or American Cancer Society and discuss their efforts to reduce tobacco use.

2. Interview a smoker concerning his/her history of smoking, efforts to stop, coughing and related symptoms, and other aspects of the addiction.

3. Investigate the city ordinances relating to smoking in your community. If there are none, get involved in getting one passed.

Self Test

1. Smoking in the United States has decreased in recent years.

   a. true   b. false

2. There is no evidence that using smokeless tobacco causes anything more serious than bad breath.

   a. true   b. false

3. Approximately _____ of all American deaths have been attributed to smoking.

   a. 5%
   b. 10%
   c. 20%
   d. 40%
   e. 50%

4. Nicotine is a powerful chemical that affects the heart, blood vessels, gastrointestinal tract, and nervous system.

   a. true   b. false

5. Carbon monoxide damages the body by

   a. reducing the oxygen-carrying capacity of the body.
   b. damaging the respiratory lining.
   c. causing emphysema.
   d. its addictive properties.

6. _____ contains the most carcinogenic substance in cigarettes.

   a. Nicotine
   b. Tar
   c. Carbon monoxide
   d. Nitrogen oxide

7. The effects of _____ and _____ probably contribute to the development of stroke and heart attacks among smokers.

   a. carbon monoxide and nicotine
   b. hydrogen cyanide and nitrogen oxide
   c. nicotine and nitrous oxide
   d. tar and hydrogen cyanide

8. Smokeless tobacco has been linked to cancer of the oral cavity, pharynx, larynx, and esophagus.

    a. true   b. false

9. Neither the length of time a person has smoked nor the amount he/she smokes has much effect on his/her risks.

    a. true   b. false

10. After the _____ in 1964, the incidence of smoking in the U.S. decreased.

    a. Korean War
    b. sexual revolution
    c. first surgeon general's report on smoking and health
    d. Cigarette Excise Tax Bill

11. It is probably the _____ that causes the addiction to cigarettes.

    a. hydrogen cyanide
    b. carbon monoxide
    c. tar
    d. nicotine

12. Smoking increases the risk of _____, as well as lung cancer, in the smoker.

    a. oral and pharyngeal cancer
    b. cancer of the esophagus
    c. cancer of the stomach, pancreas, and kidneys
    d. all of these

205

13. With emphysema or COPD, air becomes trapped in the air sacs of the lung, overinflating them and causing difficulty in breathing.

    a. true   b. false

14. _____ is/are a leading cause of death in women as well as in men.

    a. Lung cancer
    b. Kidney disease
    c. Burns
    d. Chronic bronchitis

15. Though smoking increases the risk of many diseases, the incidence of cardiovascular diseases is not much changed by smoking.

    a. true   b. false

16. Proven risks to the unborn child of pregnant mothers who smoke include all *except*

    a. prematurity.
    b. miscarriage.
    c. addiction to nicotine.
    d. low birth weight.

17. Nonsmoking family members of smokers frequently have a higher than average incidence of respiratory problems due to

    a. mainstream smoking.
    b. secondhand or passive smoking.
    c. poor hygiene.
    d. all of these

18. One of the problems of smoking is that, in order to stop, the smoker has to deny himself/herself many times each day.

    a. true   b. false

19. Though the Framingham Study is interesting, it has not had much effect on modern medicine.

    a. true   b. false

20. The U.S. government plays a strange, contradictory role in the consumption and production of tobacco.

    a. true   b. false

207

Answer Key

1. a (p. 390)
2. b (p. 390)
3. c (p. 390)
4. a (p. 391)
5. a (p. 392)
6. b (p. 392)
7. a (p. 392)
8. a (p. 392)
9. b (pp. 392-393)
10. c (TV)
11. d (p. 391)
12. d (p. 393, TV)
13. a (p. 394, TV)
14. a (p. 395, TV)
15. b (p. 396, TV)
16. c (p. 396, TV)
17. b (p. 397, TV)
18. a (TV)
19. b (TV)
20. a (TV)

LESSON 21   Smoking...Kicking The Habit

We want to help young America become tobacco-free by the year 2000. If we achieve it, that means...we will have rescued the young people of America from the preventable burden of smoking-related illness and death.

C. Everett Koop, M.D., Former Surgeon General, U.S. Public Health Service

Learning Objectives

Knowledge

Upon successful completion of all assignments in this lesson, you should be able to

1. List the most common reasons that people begin smoking.

2. Explain the reasons that smoking cessation is very difficult for most people.

3. Discuss the particular problems women are having with smoking.

4. Compare at least four of the techniques that can help a person stop smoking.

5. Discuss some of the ways that adults can discourage smoking in young people.

6. List some of the sources of help for those who wish to stop smoking.

Attitude

1. Analyze your own attitude toward smoking.

2. Describe additional laws regarding smoking that you feel should be enacted.

3. If you smoke -- STOP!

Overview

When former Surgeon General Everett Koop delivered his challenge for a smoke-free society by the year 2000, he addressed this country's greatest health need. All nonsmokers wish for a nonsmoking world -- and, incidentally, so do most smokers. Well-documented studies show that 90 percent of all smokers want to stop smoking, no matter what the reasons are for why the addiction began or continues.

In order to achieve a smoke-free society, young people must be discouraged from beginning to smoke, smokers must be helped to stop smoking, and legislation promoting clean indoor air and discouraging tobacco use must be enacted.

There are a number of different smoking cessation strategies that are sound in principle and can help smokers quit. The bottom line is that the smoker must be committed to stop smoking and must not give up if he/she is not successful on the first attempt. Smoking cessation is difficult, and different programs will work for different people. The American Lung Association and the American Cancer Society are good resources for individuals needing more information on the subject.

The U.S. government plays a very contradictory role in the matter of tobacco and smoking. On the one hand it discourages smoking because of the serious health threat to the American people, while on the other hand it supports tobacco farming and cigarette manufacturers because tobacco is an important U.S. product. If the incidence of smoking is to continue to be reduced, the government's priorities must be more in line with health priorities.

If Americans achieve Dr. Koop's smoke-free society by the year 2000, we will indeed leave an incredible legacy to future generations.

Study Assignments

Text - Chapter 15, "Tobacco," pp. 397-405

TV - Program 21, "Smoking...Kicking The Habit"

If you smoke, complete Self-Assessment, "What Makes Quitting So Hard?" on pp. 402-403 in the text.

Key Terms

aversion techniques (related to smoking cessation) (p. 401)

Text Focus Questions

1. What factors influence people to start smoking and keep smoking?

2. What types of programs are available for people who want to stop smoking? Describe each type.

3. How can we encourage a smoke-free environment?

TV Focus Questions

1. What are the special problems that women face regarding smoking?

2. What are the most common reasons people begin to smoke?

3. What are some of the psychological reasons for not starting to smoke?

4. What can teens be taught to keep them from starting to smoke?

5. What are some of the important things that adults can do to encourage young people not to start smoking?

6. What are some of the sources of help for those who want to stop smoking?

Optional Strengthening Exercise

1. Attend one of the smoking cessation programs to learn in detail how they are conducted.

Self Test

1. Many young people start smoking because

   a. their friends smoke.
   b. adults are smoking around them.
   c. smoking is a symbol of rebellion.
   d. all of these

2. People only rarely become addicted to smoking.

    a. true   b. false

3. When a person stops smoking, the following physiological changes occur *except*

    a. the heart rate drops.
    b. the blood pressure increases.
    c. the level of adrenal hormones in the bloodstream drops.
    d. the body's general arousal level drops.

4. Tobacco use can be linked with daily routines, making it important to change one's routine when trying to stop smoking.

    a. true   b. false

5. There is no risk to using smokeless tobacco.

    a. true   b. false

6. Most people who have stopped smoking have done so with professional help.

    a. true   b. false

7. The primary smoking cessation strategies include

    a. self-help.
    b. group techniques and clinics.
    c. professional therapy.
    d. behavior modification.
    e. all of these

8. Nonprofit health organizations that sponsor smoking cessation programs include the following *except*

    a. the American Lung Association.
    b. the American Cancer Society.
    c. the American Heart Association.
    d. Schick Centers.

9. When hosting a party, the host can foster a smoke-free environment by designating one room as a smoking room or only allowing smoking outdoors.

    a. true   b. false

10. Most people who smoke have no interest in stopping smoking.

    a. true   b. false

11. Even though the U.S. government has accomplished some healthy anti-smoking goals, it continues to support tobacco farming and cigarette usage.

    a. true   b. false

12. Legislation is the only way to create a smoke-free society.

    a. true   b. false

13. Women rarely smoke to assert themselves.

    a. true   b. false

214

14. Telling people about the hazards of smoking will keep them from smoking.

    a. true   b. false

15. Reasons for teenagers beginning to smoke include

    a. a dare to smoke.
    b. a cigarette given to them.
    c. parents who smoke.
    d. friends who smoke.
    e. all of these

16. Smokers who try to quit and fail should

    a. keep on trying.
    b. give up -- they probably will not stop.
    c. try another method.
    d. a and c only

17. Behavior modification techniques are frequently successful in helping with smoking cessation.

    a. true   b. false

18. The American Lung Association has been one of the leading agencies in smoking cessation and anti-smoking legislation.

    a. true   b. false

Answer Key

1. d (p. 399)
2. b (p. 399)
3. b (p. 400)
4. a (pp. 400, 403)
5. b (p. 400)
6. b (p. 401)
7. e (p. 401)
8. d (p. 401)
9. a (p. 403)
10. b (TV)
11. a (Study Guide)
12. b (Study Guide)
13. b (TV)
14. b (TV)
15. e (TV)
16. d (TV)
17. a (TV)
18. a (TV)

LESSON 22   Oh, My Aching Back

"Some excuses are real KILLERS."

National Safety Council

Learning Objectives

Knowledge

Upon successful completion of all assignments in this lesson, you should be able to

1. Summarize recent thinking about accidental and violent injuries, explaining how the agent-host-environment model is being applied to the occurrence of injuries as well as diseases.

2. Identify the most common environments in which injuries occur, typical types of injuries for each location, and the people who are likely to be injured.

3. Discuss the major types of injuries in the United States, including important factors associated with their occurrence.

4. Explain basic strategies for the prevention and control of injuries, specifying particular measures that can be taken against different types of injuries.

5. Describe important principles and procedures of emergency care that may be needed at any injury site before professional help arrives.

6. List some of the causes and symptoms of low back syndrome.

7. Discuss the practices important to the prevention of low back syndrome and other back injuries.

Attitude

1. Analyze the behaviors in your lifestyle that either contribute to or decrease your risk of accidents. Make the decision to change the negative ones.

Overview

Don't skim over this lesson because you "already know all that stuff!" The life you save by knowing or reviewing this information may be your own or that of a loved one. Accidents account for more deaths of persons ages 1 to 38 years than any other cause.

Most accidents are preventable. A large number involve alcohol and/or other drugs. Too often we falsely reason that "it couldn't happen to me." Remember when you had to have one more drink or climbed up on that shaky chair or used the electric edger when the grass was just a little wet? Then you were a candidate for a bad accident and possibly even death.

In the area of accident prevention, there has been more controversy over the use of seat belts and motorcycle helmets than over almost any other issue. Nearly everyone knows of someone who was trapped by a seat belt or who couldn't hear a car because of wearing a helmet. But what do the facts show? Ask any emergency department doctor or nurse who has seen the results of unstrapped motorists thrown through windshields and of helmetless motorcyclists.

Even the small things we take for granted can come back to haunt us. This lesson considers the "little" causes of low back syndrome, a condition that results in much pain for its victims and loss of productivity among employees.

The other vital truth in this lesson is the importance of knowing first aid and cardiopulmonary resuscitation (CPR). Have you ever been at the scene of an accident where no one knew what to do and everyone was near hysteria? This is a preventable tragedy. Anyone can and should learn first aid and CPR. In addition to being able to help someone else, you will feel much more secure about your own abilities. If you know what to do in an emergency situation, you can help others not to panic and can do what is necessary to care for the victim(s).

Study Assignment

Textbook - Chapter 16, "Injuries And Their Prevention," pp. 407-432

TV - Program 22, "Oh, My Aching Back"

Complete Self-Assessment, "How Much Excitement Can You Take?" on p. 409 in the text.

Key Terms

active prevention (p. 419)
passive prevention (p. 420)
shock (p. 426)
body mechanics (TV)
low back syndrome (TV)

Text Focus Questions

1. How does the "threshold theory" explain injuries?

2. Why is the agent-host-environment model useful in explaining why injuries happen?

3. What are the most common home injuries? Who is more likely to be injured?

4. What occupations are considered to have the greatest risks for injuries? What part do motor vehicles play in occupational injuries?

5. Describe some of the most common recreational injuries.

6. How does violence play a role in injuries?

7. What relationship does alcohol have with motor vehicle accidents? How do age and sex relate to motor vehicle accidents?

8. What are common contributing factors to injury from falls?

9. What are the other significant causes of injuries?

10. What approaches are useful in preventing injuries?

11. Compare active and passive measures for preventing injuries.

12. How can an individual lower personal risk for various injuries? Which measures are most important in preventing childhood injuries?

13. What steps can a person take to lessen the chance of being involved in violence?

14. List the basic principles of emergency care.

15. List and explain the basic procedures for emergency care.

16. What are the most common situations requiring first aid? List the steps to be taken in each situation.

TV Focus Questions

1. What are the most common causes for low back syndrome?

2. What symptoms describe low back syndrome and other back injuries?

3. What health practices are important to prevent or minimize the effects of low back syndrome?

4. How is low back syndrome treated?

Optional Strengthening Exercises

1. Contact your college or American Red Cross and take a first-aid course.

2. If you have not already done so, contact your college, American Heart Association, or American Red Cross and take a cardiopulmonary resuscitation (CPR) course.

Self Test

1. According to the _____ theory, injuries occur when a force or energy proves to be too great for a person to cope with.

   a. agent-host-environment
   b. Heimlich
   c. threshold
   d. none of these

2. The _____ theory was originally used to help explain the causes of disease but has also been used to explain why injuries occur.

   a. agent-host-environment
   b. Heimlich
   c. threshold
   d. none of these

3. _____ are more prone to injuries in the home than are others.

   a. Men
   b. Women
   c. Children
   d. Adolescents

4. A relatively small number of occupational injuries involve motor vehicles.

   a. true   b. false

5. The highest incidence of death in recreational injury is thought to be from

    a. football.
    b. skiing.
    c. sky diving.
    d. drowning.

6. Alcohol is the most important factor in motor vehicle injuries.

    a. true   b. false

7. The group most at risk for falls is

    a. children.
    b. women.
    c. the elderly.
    d. adolescents.

8. Most acts of violence are committed by

    a. women.
    b. men.
    c. gangs.
    d. adolescents.

9. The greatest failing of active prevention measures is that they depend on people to act in ways that will reduce their risk of serious injury.

    a. true   b. false

10. The best prevention against injury combines active and passive prevention.

    a. true   b. false

11. Children are not likely to drown in small pails or pots of water.

    a. true   b. false

12. It is important that everyone learn cardiopulmonary resuscitation (CPR) because

    a. a person will die in a few minutes if the oxygen supply is cut off.
    b. many lives a year could be saved.
    c. lifesaving techniques should be started immediately.
    d. it requires no special training.
    e. all except d

13. The Heimlich maneuver should be used on the choking victim if he/she cannot speak.

    a. true   b. false

14. The first step in controlling severe bleeding is to

    a. apply direct pressure over the wound.
    b. apply a tourniquet.
    c. go and get help.
    d. use the pressure point technique.

15. If a person is pale and has a faint pulse after an accident, first aid should include

    a. having the person move around.
    b. having the person lie down.
    c. giving a stimulant such as alcohol.
    d. having the person stand still.

16. Some of the more common causes of low back syndrome are

    a. severe injury.
    b. small abuses through the years.
    c. poor body mechanics.
    d. use of improper chairs.
    e. all except a

17. Backache is extremely common in the U.S. today.

    a. true   b. false

18. One of the reasons that back problems are common is probably that the discs have no blood supply.

    a. true   b. false

19. Low back syndrome usually requires surgical correction.

    a. true   b. false

20. Health practices that prevent back problems are

    a. good body mechanics.
    b. avoiding twisting the body.
    c. avoiding jogging on hard surfaces.
    d. doing exercises that strengthen the back.
    e. not starting suddenly on any exercise.
    f. all of these

Answer Key

1. c (p. 408)
2. a (p. 410)
3. c (p. 411)
4. b (p. 412)
5. d (p. 413)
6. a (p. 414)
7. c (p. 414)
8. b (p. 418)
9. a (p. 419)
10. a (p. 420)
11. b (p. 421)
12. e (p. 425, Study Guide)
13. a (p. 426)
14. a (p. 427)
15. b (p. 426)
16. e (TV)
17. a (TV)
18. a (TV)
19. b (TV)
20. c (TV)

LESSON 23   Aging: How To Die Young, As Late As Possible

But whether or not we have the chance to experience our dying, whether or not our dying becomes a "last step forward," an instrument of growth, we can -- long before we arrive at the month, the week, the day, the hour of our death -- enrich our life by remembering that we will die.

Judith Viorst, *Necessary Losses*

Learning Objectives

Knowledge

Upon successful completion of all assignments in this lesson, you should be able to

1. Describe some of the physiological changes that occur with aging.

2. Characterize the human life span in terms of healthy aging and pathological aging, and describe the common stages of growth and change in adult life.

3. Comment on the concerns of people as they age, both the functions of normal aging and problems associated with disease and more avoidable disabilities.

4. Discuss various constraints on the aging process, including genetic limits to cell reproduction, theories of aging due to physiological damage, and the effects of lifestyle.

5. Clarify ways in which people can take actions to lessen the impact of aging on their own lives and on the lives of others close to them.

6. Discuss potential needs for government intervention in solving some of the problems of the aged.

7. Describe different views of death held in different cultures and by people of different ages in our own culture.

8. Discuss the stages people may go through when confronting the fact that they are about to die and the various reactions of different individuals, depending on situational and personal factors.

9. Explore ways that others may respond to the fact that a relative or friend is about to die, including practical considerations of medical and emotional care.

10. Enumerate several preparations that people can make for their own deaths to save their loved ones from difficult dislocations and decisions during a period of grief.

11. Review the typical responses of those who are bereaved, the ways in which funeral ceremonies may help them, and other factors that may enable them to cope with and lessen their sadness over time.

Attitude

1. Give specific examples of signs that attitudes toward the elderly are changing.

2. Describe ways in which the wisdom and experience of older people can be put to better use.

228

3. Describe some of the images of death seen on television and discuss the presence or lack of realism.

4. Debate the two sides of the issue of telling dying adults of their impending death. Do the same in the case of dying children.

Overview

Live long enough and you will surely become elderly and die. Some die before they become old. Aging and death are normal, inevitable parts of life. Intellectually, we accept all these statements as true, but can we emotionally accept the idea that we ourselves and our loved ones will undergo this process? These are issues that you have to come to grips with, sooner or later, in order to lead a full, healthy, happy life.

Unfortunately the elderly are too frequently portrayed as testy, miserable people living in nursing homes. In reality this is far from the truth. Even though slowed and subject to some of the aggravations and chronic diseases of aging, most people have the capacity to spend their "golden years" happily independent and in relative good health. Lifestyle decisions you make now will significantly influence what happens around the age of 65 and beyond.

This lesson also vividly demonstrates the role that government, community, family, and friends can play in improving the quality of life of the older person. Every individual should take a proactive position to make certain that aging individuals are not forced into becoming second-class citizens.

Death comes to all, whether we accept it or not. Unlike on television where the hero "blows away" 20 or so villains without any emotion, death is an intense personal experience. When life was simpler, people died at home surrounded by their family and were buried under the oak tree on the hill. Today, we must deal with death in intensive care units or with organ transplantation, "pulling the plug," and other factors not always clearly understood. We must never lose sight of the need for the dying patient and that person's family to work through the stages of grief in their own way.

Modern technology has brought many new ethical issues into focus. Two of these -- the issue of what constitutes death and the issue of organ transplantation -- have generated more interest as technological advances have occurred. It is generally accepted that brain death, or loss of electrical activity in the brain, is the measure of death. When brain death occurs, life-sustaining efforts become postponements of death rather than methods of sustaining life. It is important to understand this concept if you are to make value decisions about organ donation for transplant purposes. Reports of successful organ transplants increase every year, but, sadly, many die for lack of a needed organ. The clergy of major religions have accepted the concept of organ transplants as positive and good. Now if we are to follow their lead, we must make decisions to ensure that organs will be available for those who need them. The impending death of a loved one is not the time to develop a value system about this issue.

Take from this lesson an understanding and caring attitude for the aged population. Learn how to live by learning how to face death.

Study Assignments

Textbook - Chapter 17, "Lifestyle And Growing Older," pp. 435-457 and Chapter 18, "Dying and Death," pp. 459-481

TV - Program 23, "Aging: How To Die Young, As Late As Possible"

Complete the Self-Assessment, "How Anxious Are You About Death?" on p. 463 in the text.

Key Terms

normal aging (p. 436, TV)
pathological aging (p. 436)
gerontology (p. 436)
life span (p. 436)
life expectancy (p. 436)
osteoporosis (p. 436)
diabetes (p. 445)
arthritis (p. 445)
Alzheimer's disease (p. 445, TV)
thanatology (p. 459)
clinical death (p. 459)
brain death (p. 459)
euthanasia (p. 472)
passive euthanasia (p. 472)
active euthanasia (p. 472)
mourning (p. 473)
bereavement (p. 475)
grief (p. 475)

Text Focus Questions

1. How does normal aging occur? Include the life stages in the discussion.

2. What are some of the concerns of growing older? How do appearance, body tissue, and body function change?

3. What chronic diseases are more common with aging? Discuss the nature of these diseases.

4. Why do we age? Describe some of the theories on aging.

5. What factors are important in maintaining health and well-being through the aging process?

6. How does the meaning of death differ from individual to individual and in different age groups?

7. Discuss the progress of an individual through the five stages of coping with death as described by Kubler-Ross.

8. What are some of the psychological responses of the dying?

9. Why do people commit suicide? How can suicide affect the survivors?

10. Why is home care or hospice care preferable for the dying person if it is possible?

11. What important practical decisions should be made well in advance of death?

12. Discuss the ethics and morality of euthanasia.

13. How can the process of mourning and the funeral service be helpful to survivors?

14. In what ways do patterns of bereavement differ and why do these differences occur?

TV Focus Questions

1. Discuss some of the physiological changes that take place with aging.

2. Describe some of the financial problems of the elderly.

3. What role might the federal government take in helping with some of the problems of the elderly?

4. Contrast Alzheimer's disease with the normal aging process.

5. How can the family and society help the elderly enjoy a better life?

Optional Strengthening Exercises

1. Arrange an interview with a geriatric nurse and discuss the life of the aged person.

2. Visit with an aged person living in a nursing home and one living independently. Compare their lifestyles, health condition, and quality of life.

3. Talk with health professionals, lawyers, and clergy concerning the idea of passive euthanasia and/or organ transplantation.

4. Talk with professionals working at a suicide prevention or crisis center about the effect of suicide on the family.

5. Visit a funeral home and discuss with a staff member how funeral arrangements are made.

Self Test

1. The process of physical, mental, emotional, and social change experienced throughout life is

   a. senescence.
   b. aging.
   c. maturation.
   d. developmental tasks.

2. _____ refers to certain biological processes that are time related rather than being a function of disease, injury, or stress.

   a. Gerontology
   b. Thanatology
   c. Pathological aging
   d. Normal aging

3. According to psychologist Erik Erikson, the _____ period is a time of transition, when most people are experimenting with new roles and struggling with decisions about the future.

   a. young adulthood
   b. middle age
   c. adult entry
   d. older adulthood

4. Older people frequently need fewer calories than, but as much nutrition as, younger people.

   a. true   b. false

5. Normal physiological signs of aging include

   a. wrinkling of skin.
   b. stiffening of joints.
   c. decrease in hearing.
   d. all of these

6. Few older people have any interest in sex.

   a. true   b. false

7. Chronic diseases that are somewhat debilitating but not life threatening frequently plague the elderly.

   a. true   b. false

8. Because regular exercise in the aging person causes osteoporosis, it should be avoided.

   a. true   b. false

9. Anyone who lives long enough is certain to have some degree of Alzheimer's disease.

   a. true   b. false

10. Although Alzheimer's disease is not curable, some of the treatment strategies include

   a. daily exercise and social contact.
   b. proper diet and prescription medicines.
   c. social contact.
   d. all of these

11. Proponents of the "genetic limits" theory of aging believe that

    a. ndividuals are programmed to live a specific length of time.
    b chemical wastes accumulate in the body.
    c the body is like a complex piece of machinery that wears out.
    d tissues containing collagen stiffen and become more brittle.

12. The free radical theory holds that substances released by polyunsaturated fats produce chemical reactions that alter and damage body cells.

    a. true   b. false

13. Lifestyle decisions that impact our later years are

    a. regular exercise and diet.
    b. diet, regular exercise, smoking, and social contacts.
    c. smoking, regular exercise, and social contacts.
    d. social contacts, diet, and smoking.

14. Most old people live in nursing homes and are unhappy.

    a. true   b. false

15. The community and society as a whole have a role in solving some of the problems of the elderly.

    a. true   b. false

16. The absence of heartbeat and the cessation of breathing are termed _____, and the absence of brain activity for 24 hours, even though breathing and circulation are maintained, is termed _____.

    a. death, clinical death
    b. brain death, death
    c. clinical death, brain death
    d. none of these

17. Fear of death is often associated with the fear of nonbeing or the loss of everything.

    a. true   b. false

18. Children deal with death far more easily than adults do.

    a. true   b. false

19. The order in which an individual passes through Kubler-Ross' stages of dying is

    a. depression, anger, bargaining, denial, acceptance.
    b. denial, anger, acceptance, bargaining, depression.
    c. denial, anger, bargaining, depression, acceptance.
    d. anger, denial, bargaining, depression, acceptance.

20. Belligerent outbursts, hostile attitudes, and envy are normal parts of the _____ stage.

    a. anger
    b. denial
    c. bargaining
    d. depression

21. The individual reaches the peaceful stage of _____ when he/she may prefer nonverbal communication from friends and loved ones.

    a. denial
    b. bargaining
    c. depression
    d. acceptance

22. Suicide is usually a desperate response to depression and having lost the will to live.

    a. true   b. false

23. Hospice care differs from hospital care in that the former

    a. does not attempt to cure the patient.
    b. has a lower quality of care.
    c. takes place in smaller facilities.
    d. offers only organ transplants.

24. It is best just to tell the dying patient that things will be fine if you don't know what to say.

    a. true   b. false

25. A _____ is a legal document that specifies how a person wishes his or her property distributed after death.

    a. living will
    b. trust
    c. court order
    d. will

26. Withdrawing the life support system from a vegetative, comatose patient is

   a. murder.
   b. active euthanasia.
   c. passive euthanasia.
   d. illegal.

27. Though funerals are an expected ritual in our society, they serve no particularly useful purpose to the survivors.

   a. true   b. false

28. Physical symptoms and guilt are frequently seen as abnormal grief patterns.

   a. true   b. false

29. The person who has lost a loved one frequently lashes out with hostility and resentment, very normal reactions.

   a. true   b. false

30. "Normal" grief usually lasts at least three or four years.

   a. true   b. false

Answer Key

1. b (TV)
2. d (p. 436)
3. c (p. 438)
4. a (p. 441)
5. d (p. 441, TV)
6. b (p. 441)
7. a (pp. 443-444, TV)
8. b (p. 445)
9. b (p. 445, TV)
10. d (pp. 446-447, TV)
11. a (p. 448)
12. a (p. 449, TV)
13. b (pp. 450-451, TV)
14. b (p. 455, TV)
15. a (TV)
16. c (p. 459)
17. a (pp. 460-461)
18. b (pp. 461-462)
19. c (p. 464)
20. a (p. 464)
21. d (p. 464)
22. a (p. 466)
23. a (p. 469)
24. b (p. 470)
25. d (p. 470)
26. b (p. 472)
27. b (p. 474)
28. a (p. 475)
29. a (p. 476)
30. b (p. 478)

LESSON 24   For Relief Of...Take Two

"Nine out of ten doctors recommend..."

An overused, misleading advertising gimmick

Learning Objectives

Knowledge

Upon successful completion of all assignments in this lesson, you should be able to

1. Explain the importance of being health activated and describe some of the basic attitudes, judgments, and types of action characteristic of health activation.

2. Describe important information needed for medical self-care, such as normal physiological data, the way to organize a medicine chest, the importance of physical examinations, and criteria for seeking medical help.

3. Compare the so-called good headaches with bad headaches.

4. Explain tension, migraine, and cluster headaches, including the primary cause of pain, symptoms, and treatment.

5. Describe modifications of lifestyle recommended to decrease headaches and steps in treating headaches.

6. List headache symptoms indicating that there may be more serious problems present.

241

7. Describe some of the various types of medical quackery prevalent in the United States.

Attitude

1. Review your own use of over-the-counter drugs, including number and type taken, frequency of use, whether they live up to claims, and whether they are really needed. Take action on your findings.

2. Evaluate your attitude toward drug advertising and decide whether your attitudes are realistic. Are you easily "sold," or are you overly suspicious of all medications? Take action on your findings.

Overview

Most Americans purchase and use over-the-counter drugs on a regular basis. Most of these drugs are reasonably effective if used for what they are intended -- relieving symptoms. Very few are designed to cure anything. Problems arise when these drugs are misused. Any condition that lingers or increases in severity should be evaluated by a physician, not treated with more over-the-counter drugs.

The consumer should also be aware that many over-the-counter drugs are actually the same drug packaged differently. For example, no matter what company makes aspirin, it is the same product. It has to be, or it could not be called aspirin. These drugs are not without dangers either. Bad reactions can accompany over-the-counter preparations just as they can occur with prescription drugs. In fact, many over-the-counter preparations contain ingredients that increase the chances for side effects.

Of all ailments treated with over-the-counter drugs, headache is probably the most common. Aspirin is quite effective in treating certain types of headaches, but it is important to understand the symptoms of a simple headache and be able to recognize signs that something more serious is occurring. There also are nonmedical solutions for headache sufferers, such as avoiding certain foods, learning to relax, and avoiding the glaring rays of sunlight. All help to prevent or decrease the pain of headaches.

Even in an enlightened society, medical quackery and false or questionable advertising flourishes. The reasons for their existence are clear: people are desperate for a cure where no cure exists; people tend to believe anything they read or see on television; and the lure of being young, slim, and beautiful is very strong. The result? Enormous amounts of money are wasted on useless and dangerous drugs, beauty aids, and treatments. Consumers should look at advertising and treatment claims with a wary eye. Check out claims with your physician, pharmacist, local medical society, or the Food and Drug Administration. Legitimate medicines and treatments can tolerate this kind of scrutiny. Quackery cannot.

Study Assignment

Textbook - Chapter 19, "Medical Care In America," pp. 483-492

TV - Program 24, "For The Relief Of...Take Two"

Key Terms

generic name (p. 486)
migraine headache (TV)
cluster headache (TV)
tension headache (TV)

Text Focus Questions

1. What are the advantages of being a health-activated person?

2. How does one judge what can be self-treated and what requires medical attention?

3. How can a person choose an over-the-counter medication to alleviate certain minor symptoms?

4. What are the most common patterns of medical quackery?

5. What information must be monitored to be able to care for one's own health?

6. What safety measures are important for the storage of medications at home?

7. Why is a regular physical exam important? What are the usual components of a physical exam?

8. What symptoms indicate the need for professional help?

TV Focus Questions

1. What are some of the typical symptoms of the types of headaches where there is no tissue destruction?

2. Differentiate between tension, migraine, and cluster headaches in symptoms and treatment.

3. What modifications in lifestyle can be made to lessen the occurrence and effects of headaches?

4. What symptoms indicate that there may be more serious causes for a headache and that medical evaluation is needed?

Optional Strengthening Exercises

1. Take an inventory of all the over-the-counter drugs in your home. Check the expiration dates and discard any that are out-of-date. Do the same for prescription drugs. Are they still safe to use?

2. Note television advertising of over-the-counter medical and health products. Do you see examples of quackery?

3. In a visit to your pharmacy, read the labels of a number of over-the-counter preparations. Select at least two or three designed to treat one condition. Carefully read the labels. Do you find similarities? Differences? How many ingredients are listed? What is the cost of each medicine?

4. Ask your pharmacist for the price of some prescription drugs by manufacturer's name and by generic name. Is there a significant cost difference?

Self Test

1. A truly health-activated person has little need for health professionals.

   a. true   b. false

2. A health professional should be consulted when a medical problem exceeds

   a. a person's skills.
   b. the tools or information available.
   c. the support to deal with it.
   d. all of these
   e. none of these

3. Most over-the-counter drugs

   a. cure disease.
   b. treat symptoms.
   c. are inexpensive.
   d. are useless.

4. It is completely the consumer's decision whether to choose a generic drug.

   a. true   b. false

5. Medical quackery is dangerous as well as irritating.

   a. true   b. false

6. Scare tactics used in advertising can be examples of

   a. illegal advertising.
   b. subliminal advertising.
   c. quackery.
   d. none of these

7. Migraine headaches frequently cause

    a. pain on one side of the head.
    b. a change in vision on the opposite side.
    c. nausea.
    d. balance difficulty.
    e. weakness.
    f. a, b, and c only
    g. all of these

8. Tension headaches are usually relieved by aspirin and relaxation.

    a. true   b. false

9. Headaches are rarely caused by stress or depression.

    a. true   b. false

10. Lifestyle modifications that are useful in decreasing headaches are

    a. wearing polarized sunglasses.
    b. decreasing the use of nitrites, MSG, and alcohol.
    c. avoiding red wine and chocolate.
    d. all of these
    e. none of these

11. _____, _____, and _____ are basic measurements of an individual's physiological data that can be simply measured by the person.

    a. Temperature, cholesterol level, pulse
    b. Temperature, tonometry, EKG
    c. Temperature, pulse, respiration
    d. Blood pressure, pulse, cholesterol level

12. It is permissible to put medicine in an unlabeled bottle if it is only going to be in that container for a short time.

    a. true   b. false

13. The optimum frequency of physical exams is

    a. once a year.
    b. once every two years.
    c. once every five years.
    d. dependent on the individual's age and health status.

14. Regular physical exams are much more important than regular dental and eye exams.

    a. true   b. false

15. It is important to seek professional help immediately if _____ occur(s).

    a. severe pain
    b. cold sweats
    c. unconsciousness or disorientation
    d. all of the above

Answer Key

1. b (p. 484)   9. b (TV)
2. d (p. 484)   10. d (TV)
3. b (p. 486)   11. c (p. 487)
4. b (p. 486)   12. b (p. 490)
5. a (p. 487)   13. d (p. 491)
6. c (p. 487)   14. b (p. 492)
7. f (TV)   15. d (p. 492)
8. b (p. 519)

LESSON 25   How To Talk To Your Doctor/Your Patient

Patients' Rights include

1. *The right to humane care and treatment,*
2. *The right to competent treatment,*
3. *The right to accurate information...the right to participate appropriately in decisions regarding their health care,*
4. *The right to confidentiality regarding disclosures and records,*
5. *The right to information regarding the scope and availability of services,*
6. *The right to information regarding fees-for-services,*
7. *The right to full information regarding appropriate channels for expressing grievances and making evaluations,*
8. *The right to know organizational policies regarding experimental research without jeopardizing access to care.*

American College Health Association, *Recommended Standards and Practices for a College Health Program, 1984*

Learning Objectives

Knowledge

Upon successful completion of all assignments in this lesson, you should be able to

1. Compare and contrast the different types of medical help available in the United States today, indicating factors to consider when choosing among them.

2. Discuss different ways in which health care is financed in the United States.

3. Analyze some of the advantages and disadvantages of the available systems of health care financing.

4. Discuss the reasons for lack of trust and even hostility between physicians and their patients.

5. Describe the medical school's role in the negative doctor/patient relationship.

6. Discuss the ways in which positive physician/patient relationships can be fostered.

Attitude

1. Examine your own relationship with your physician and evaluate how you and the doctor could make it more positive.

Overview

As a patient you have certain rights that guarantee high-quality health care. Your physician also has rights. Both you and your physician enter into the physician/patient relationship with various responsibilities and expectations. If any of these aspects breaks down, the relationship can become negative. The most common problem arising in the physician/ patient relationship is a failure to communicate. For example, the patient feels the physician should "know" what the patient is thinking; the physician assumes the patient "knows" how to take the prescribed medication. Both parties blame the other and everyone loses -- except the lawyers in the malpractice suit that may follow.

The time for patient and physician to discuss their relationship is before anything serious occurs. A routine physical exam gives both an opportunity to talk and negotiate expectations.

This lesson also discusses the importance of health insurance. At that very point in their lives when young adults think they can't afford health insurance, they need it the most. Even a relatively minor emergency surgery or illness can cost thousands of dollars. Health insurance options abound -- take time to find the one that's right for you.

Study Assignment

Textbook - Chapter 19, "Medical Care In America," pp. 493-507

TV - Program 25, "How To Talk To Your Doctor/Your Patient"

Key Terms

basic health insurance (p. 503)
major medical insurance (p. 503)
disability insurance (p. 503)
group policies (p. 503)
individual policies (p. 503)
Medicare (p. 503)
Medicaid (p. 505)
family practitioner (TV)

Text Focus Questions

1. How does a person or family choose a physician? How does an individual evaluate the health care being provided?

2. How does an individual evaluate a hospital or clinic?

3. What other complementary approaches to health care exist? Describe each one.

4. Compare and contrast the various types of health insurance including Medicare and Medicaid.

5. What are the advantages and disadvantages of health maintenance organizations?

TV Focus Questions

1. How does a lack of trust develop between patient and physician?

2. In what way can the training of the physician contribute to the negative relationship?

3. In what way can patients' expectations and behavior contribute to the negative climate of the relationship?

4. What can the physician and the patient do to improve their relationship?

Optional Strengthening Exercises

1. Investigate several health insurance plans (including Medicare) and compare benefits, costs, deductibles, and other aspects.

2. Interview several physicians and several of your friends. Ask both groups about their expectations of a physician/patient relationship and compare their responses.

Self Test

1. Because of the large number of skilled physicians, there is no shortage of doctors in the United States today.

    a. true   b. false

2. A friend's recommendation is the best way to choose a physician.

    a. true   b. false

3. The public library can be a good source in finding information about a physician *except*

    a. educational background.
    b. training.
    c. awards and credentials.
    d. fees.

4. One of the reasons the physician/patient relationship is unsatisfactory is that

   a. lifestyles are causing diseases physicians can't cure.
   b. patients have unreasonable expectations.
   c time, pressure, and responsibility prevent a good relationship.
   d. understanding is lacking on both sides.
   e. personalities clash.
   f. all except b
   g. all except e
   h. all of these

5. A physician's education may actually contribute to a negative doctor/patient relationship in that

   a. complex technical knowledge overshadows "bedside manner" training.
   b. most training involves acute care medicine, not "everyday" illnesses.
   c. the medical terminology taught makes it difficult to learn to explain things in ordinary lay terms.
   d. a and b only
   e. b and c only
   f. all of these

6. It is important for the patient and the physician to clearly discuss their expectations of each other.

   a. true   b. false

7. To improve relationships with patients, physicians should

    a. show respect and concern.
    b. meet patients in the office before the examination.
    c. write down complicated instructions.
    d. discuss fees whenever there are questions about them.
    e. personally be available to the patient at all times.
    f. all of these
    g. all except d
    h. all except e

8. Patients should be certain that they

    a. take medication as prescribed.
    b. follow through on agreed-upon diagnostic tests.
    c. truthfully ask and answer questions.
    d. come on time for scheduled appointments.
    e. pay their bills on time.
    f. all except c
    g. all of these

9. The best hospitals are often teaching hospitals affiliated with medical schools.

    a. true   b. false

10. The hospitalized patient should take _____ role in making decisions about hospital care.

    a. a passive
    b. no
    c. an active
    d. none of these

11. A physician who was taught manipulation as a technique that helps the body's natural resistance to disease is called a/an

   a. medical doctor.
   b. osteopathic physician.
   c. orthopedist.
   d. doctor of podiatric medicine.

12. In _____, the theory is that there are fields of energy that flow through the body, and if needles are inserted at the proper points in these fields, it is possible to restore a person's health.

   a. acupuncture
   b. neuropathy
   c. chiropractic
   d. osteopathy

13. Usually there is no limit to what will be paid for by basic health insurance.

   a. true   b. false

14. _____ is/are government subsidized health insurance coverage(s) for special populations.

   a. Blue Cross and Blue Shield
   b. Health maintenance organizations
   c. Disability insurance
   d. Medicare and Medicaid

15. The advantage of belonging to a health maintenance organization (HMO) is that once the premium is paid, there are only minimal costs to the patient -- no matter how serious the illness.

   a. true   b. false

Answer Key

1. b (p. 494)
2. b (pp. 494-496)
3. d (p. 495)
4. g (TV)
5. f (TV)
6. a (TV)
7. h (TV)
8. g (TV)
9. a (p. 498)
10. c (p. 498)
11. b (p. 500)
12. a (pp. 500-501)
13. b (p. 503)
14. d (pp. 503, 505)
15. a (p. 505)

LESSON 26 A Healthy Environment

One summer night, out on a flat headland, all but surrounded by the waters of the bay, the horizons were remote and distant rims on the edge of space. Millions of stars blazed in darkness, and on the far shore a few lights burned in cottages. Otherwise there was no reminder of human life. My companion and I were alone with the stars: the misty river of the Milky Way flowing across the sky, the patterns of the constellations standing out bright and clear, a blazing planet low on the horizon.

It occurred to me that if this were a sight that could be seen only once in a century, this little headland would be thronged with spectators. But it can be seen many scores of nights in any year, and so the lights burned in the cottages and the inhabitants probably gave not a thought to the beauty overhead; and because they could see it almost any night, perhaps they never will.

Rachel Carson, *The Sense of Wonder*

Learning Objectives

Knowledge

Upon successful completion of all assignments in this lesson, you should be able to

1. Describe the major types of atmospheric pollution that affect local environments and the measures that are being taken and can be taken to alleviate them.

2. Describe the different types of pollution that affect the nation's water resources and explain how society is currently attempting to deal with them.

3. Describe the problem of solid waste, how to clean up sites that were polluted in the past, and how to prevent these problems from occurring in the future.

4. Assess the problems being caused by pollution and poor use of resources on a global scale and describe ways in which these problems might be addressed.

5. Explain and evaluate types of individual and collective action that can be taken to address environmental problems.

Attitude

1. Inventory your use of environmental resources.

2. Examine your own feelings toward nuclear energy.

Overview

Through recent history humankind has used the environment as though it were infinite and possessed resources that were unending. Now, "the moment of truth" has come. Pollution, the depletion of natural resources, the extinction of many species, and human health problems have made us realize that this planet's finite resources *must* be preserved and nurtured.

There are some major efforts under way to clean up our world and reverse the decline of the environment. It is already too late for some species; it is to be hoped that the rest of us won't have the same fate.

Protecting the environment is the responsibility of everyone. All of us must do our part to preserve the earth's precious resources. Environmental agencies cannot do it all, nor can they do it alone.

Throughout this course we have discussed individual responsibility for maintaining health. The same thought applies to caring for the environment. Now's the time to do what we must to leave future generations a safe, healthy place in which to live.

Study Assignment

Textbook - Chapter 20, "Health And The Environment," pp. 509-530

Complete Self-Assessment, "How Knowledgeable Are You About The Environment?" on pp. 512-513 in the text.

Key Terms

pollution (p. 509)
ozone (p. 511)
carrying capacity (p. 514)
chlorinated hydrocarbons (p. 514)
polychlorinated biphenyls (PCBs) (p. 515)
acid rain (p. 515)
eutrophication (p. 516)
thermal pollution (p. 516)
ozone layer (p. 520)
biodegradation (p. 526)

Text Focus Questions

1. How does the air become polluted? What are the consequences of atmospheric pollution?

2. What is being done to improve air quality?

3. Why has water pollution become such a critical issue? What are the types of pollutants adding to the problem?

4. How are we working toward improving water quality?

5. What are some examples of pollution of the land?

6. Compare the handling of hazardous wastes with that of non-hazardous wastes.

7. What are some of the critical global environmental issues facing us? Why is each important?

8. What are some of the alternative energy sources? Discuss advantages and disadvantages of each.

9. What personal and cooperative actions must be taken to protect the environment for the future?

Optional Strengthening Exercise

1. Interview local representatives of environmental protection agencies and find out what the major environmental problems in your area are and what is being done to combat these.

Self Test

1. Pollution has become a critical problem not only because of its effects on the physical environment but also because of its effects on the people who live in the environment.

   a. true   b. false

2. The major air pollutant(s) is/are

   a. carbon monoxide.
   b. ozone.
   c. hydrocarbon and nitrogen oxides.
   d. sulfur oxides and particulates.
   e. all of these

3. Air pollution affects not only our health but also the economy in damage to plants, animals, and products.

   a. true   b. false

4. The _____ sets limits on major pollutants and mandates reductions in automobile and factory emissions.

   a. U.S. Public Health Service
   b. U.S. Citizens for a Safe Environment
   c. Nuclear Regulatory Agency
   d. U.S. Environmental Protection Agency

5. The major source(s) of water pollution is/are

   a. pesticides and other chemicals.
   b. acid rain.
   c. sewage and organic matter.
   d. thermal pollution.
   e. all of these

6. Unfortunately it takes generations to clean up any lake or river that is polluted.

   a. true   b. false

7. A major problem in the United States is uncontrolled dumping of hazardous wastes.

   a. true   b. false

8. Most hazardous wastes are handled at centralized, specialized landfills.

   a. true   b. false

9. The measures most useful in solving the problems of non-hazardous wastes include

   a. expanding landfills.
   b. burning trash.
   c. recycling.
   d. none of these
   e. all of these

10. The earth is protected from harmful ultraviolet light by the

    a. smog.
    b. air.
    c. CFGs.
    d. ozone layer.

11. There is still controversy about global warming or the "greenhouse effect."

    a. true   b. false

12. At present, forests in the world are being replanted as fast as they are being cut down.

    a. true   b. false

13. There is no way to reverse the trend of increased population and resource overuse in the United States.

    a. true   b. false

14. If the world is to survive, we must learn how to use land more wisely and restore lands that have become unproductive.

    a. true   b. false

15. It is becoming more important to increase use of forms of energy other than fossil fuels.

    a. true   b. false

16. The greatest danger(s) of nuclear energy production is/are

    a. air pollution.
    b. the escape of radioactivity.
    c. the problems of finding safe ways to dispose of toxic and radioactive wastes.
    d. all of these

17. Although the United States has less than 5 percent of the total world population, it is the largest consumer of energy and natural resources.

    a. true   b. false

18. Protecting the environment is a business and industry responsibility rather than a personal one.

    a. true   b. false

19. Protecting the environment requires many hard decisions and trade-offs.

    a. true   b. false

20. Some of the most active volunteer organizations working on environmental concerns are all of these *except*

    a. the Sierra Club.
    b. the Wilderness Society.
    c. the World Wildlife Fund.
    d. Greenpeace.
    e. the EPA.

Answer Key

1. a (p. 509)
2. e (pp. 510-511)
3. a (pp. 510-511)
4. d (p. 511)
5. e (pp. 514-516)
6. b (p. 516)
7. a (p. 517)
8. b (p. 519)
9. c (p. 519)
10. d (p. 520)
11. a (p. 520)
12. b (p. 521)
13. b (p. 522)
14. a (p. 522)
15. a (p. 523)
16. d (p. 524)
17. a (p. 525)
18. b (p. 526)
19. a (p. 527)
20. e (p. 528)